Pacific knits & eats

susan gehringer

Enjoy the adventure!
Susan

Family Friends
Food & Fun
Kevin

© 2018 grist creative llc

All rights reserved. No part of this book may be reproduced, stored in any retrieval system, or transmitted in any form or by any means, mechanical, electronic, photocopying, recording, or otherwise, without written permission of the publisher. Patterns and recipes are for personal use only and may not be used to make items for sale.

grist CREATIVE

grist creative llc
Redmond, Washington
www.gristcreative.com
hello@gristcreative.com

Every effort has been made to ensure the information in this book is correct. The publisher, authors and contributors are not responsible for any injuries, losses, or damages that may result from the use of information in this book. The Health Department would like you to know that eating raw or undercooked food may increase your risk of food borne illness.

Printed in the United States of America
ISBN: 978-0-9906582-3-8

Pacific
knits&eats

susan gehringer

contents

the adventure continues	vi
bespoke	1
gambol shawl + scarf	7
The Artful Ewe	
orange-zest raisin french toast + sourdough waffles	17
Block Wines	
dyed in the wool	25
fibonacci lounge socks	31
The Homestead Hobbyist	
carrot-apple-ginger soup + grilled sandwiches	37
Sonoris Wines	
wild	43
maverick cowl + scarf	49
grist creative	
empanadas with mole + queso blanco béchamel	55
Damsel Cellars	

natural **65**

bitterroot sweater + vest + hat 71
Serenity Sheep Farm

scallywag stacked tostadas 83
Dusted Valley

speckle **89**

cassiopeia cowl + loop 95
NanoStitch Labs

lemongrass pork roast 101
Sparkman Cellars

gradient **107**

sunspray shawl 113
Canon Hand Dyes

citrus caramel pears 121
Adrice Wines

more **127**

stitches 128
gratitude 131
links 132

the adventure continues

This book is all about color—colorful yarn, colorful food, colorful wine, and the colorful personalities of all the people we meet along the way. From natural to speckled to gradient to bespoke, color speaks to us in all aspects of our lives.

We had such a wonderful experience working on **Northwest knits + eats** and had so many ideas that couldn't be contained in a single book that we decided to continue the theme and focus on color. **Pacific knits + eats** expands on the knitting + food + wine concept by adding options. It's not always easy to picture a knitted piece in a different color or to imagine a meal paired with a different wine, so we've done a bit of the work here—many of the designs are shown in multiple color options and the recipes offer some alternate presentations or wine ideas in red, white, and rosé. It's all about choice and experimentation and fun!

We continue to focus on our home base of the Pacific Northwest (specifically Northwest Washington) with yarn companies and wineries in Washington and Oregon within a day trip away, and one farm a bit farther afield needing a road trip to Montana.

We are fortunate to live in the heart of Washington wine country—well, the heart of the tasting rooms anyway—with Oregon wine country only a short road trip away. Living where we do gives us the opportunity to sample and enjoy a wide variety of Washington and Oregon wines.

No tasting adventure is complete without a discussion of flavors and potential food pairings and those very stimulating discussions are often the starting point for our favorite new recipes.

We are also lucky to be surrounded by brilliant people doing amazing things with yarn. The care and imagination that goes into artist-dyed yarn is truly inspiring. Sometimes that perfect color is all it takes to get the design ideas popping, sometimes it is the abundant natural beauty of the Northwest, and at other times it is the warmth of the people here that get the ideas flowing.

Please join us on our continuing journey. Whether you explore in person or from your armchair, we hope this book encourages you to enjoy the beauty and flavors of the Northwest.

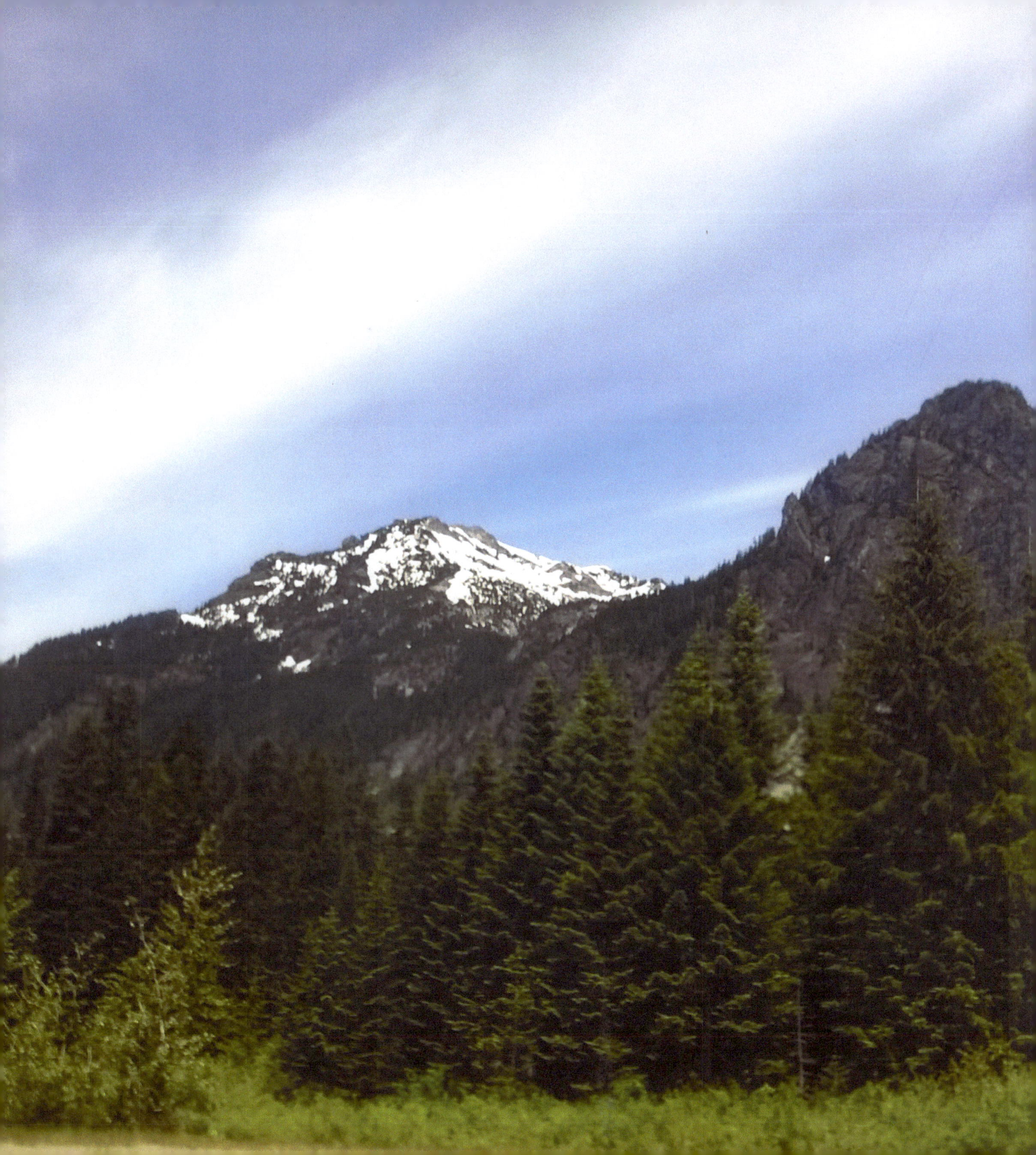

bespoke

We all have our own favorite colors, textures, and flavors. Knitting our own clothing and cooking our own food allows us to create wonderful bespoke garments and meals.

on pins & needles

Every knitter is unique. One amazing way to explore our individuality is to create our own yarn. Spinners do this all the time and so can you—no spinning wheel or inclination required. Creating a bespoke yarn is easily accomplished by holding two or more strands of yarn together while knitting…and this is where the fun begins!

For the gambol shawl, I wanted to embody the feeling of warmth and community I get every time I wander over to the Olympic Peninsula to visit The Artful Ewe. Nestled in the quaint seaside town of Port Gamble, a scenic ferry ride and short drive from Seattle, is a small shop that saturates the senses and satisfies the fiber-lover's quest for inspiration and sanctuary. The Artful Ewe is filled with fabulous fiber and yarn hand-dyed by owner Heidi Dascher. Spinners, felters, knitters, and weavers will revel in the luxurious textures and glorious colors, and be inspired by all the samples. Wander to the back of the shop just past the loom and woodstove and find a chair among the regular community of knitters that congregate here in the library nook—the "tribe" is always willing to offer opinions

and advice. Come, sit and knit, peruse the wonderful library, visit with fellow enthusiasts, or just simply be.

on the menu

Early in our wine self-education, we were lucky enough to discover Full Pull Wines. Owner Paul Zitarelli does the arduous work of tasting a wide variety of wines from the Pacific Northwest and around the world, securing parcels of interesting wines, and then sharing these wines with his mailing list. Here we had a curated entrée to wines from around the world—without the overwhelming confusion of facing a huge wall of unknown wine in a shop—and with the added bonus of Paul's mouth-watering descriptions. We were hooked! Our wine closet grew along with our knowledge and for that we are truly grateful.

There is a Zitarelli house rule of always having sparkling wine on hand. A few years ago, when Paul started his own house label focusing on terroir and single varietals from individual "blocks," we expected there would be a sparkling wine and knew that it would be special. We eagerly awaited the bubbles.

This gorgeous pale pink sparkling wine is made from Pinot Noir grapes grown at a cool Yakima Valley vineyard, a rare occurence of Pinot Noir in Washington State, and-crafted by Treveri Cellars. It is definitely worth a taste (or two)!

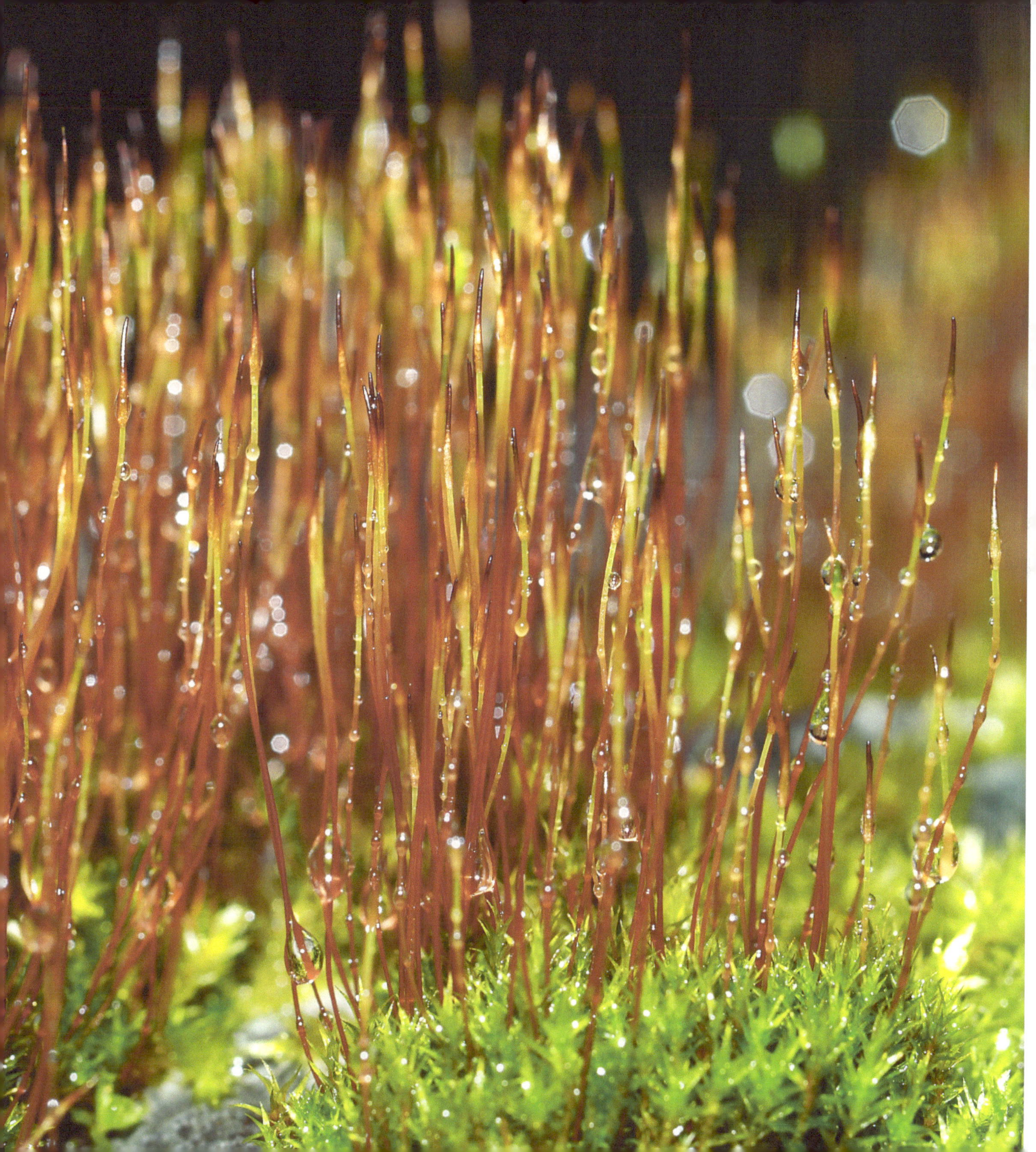

bespoke

on pins & needles

Sometimes a yarn or a journey or a community inspires a pattern and with this shawl it was a combination of all three!

A strand of merino/yak/silk yarn plus one of silk/mohair were selected to create a bespoke yarn that represents individuals joining together as a community.

The "new" yarn needed some swatching to find just the right gauge and stitches to evoke the story of growth and change and community that I wanted to tell with this design. The final pattern is reminiscent of a meandering and joyful journey.

The movement of the pattern is very rhythmic and flows smoothly once it is set up, just like setting out on an expedition that becomes more relaxing and interesting as it evolves. So, pour a favorite beverage, pull up a chair, and join in this pleasurable knitting voyage.

gambol

Size
Scarf: 9" x 80" (22 x 200 cm)
Shawl: 17" x 71" (40 x 180 cm)

Yarn
Two strands of yarn are held together:
Fingering weight, 800 (1600) yds plus
Lace weight, 800 (1600) yds

Shown in The Artful Ewe Lotus (400 yds / ~3.5 oz), 2 (4) skeins and The Artful Ewe Kid Mohair Lace (500 yds / ~1.9 oz), 2 (4) skeins.

Gauge and Needles
20 sts & 27 rows = 4" / 10 cm in stockinette after blocking using US 6-9 (4-5.5mm) or size needed to get gauge.

Gauge is not critical for this project; a different gauge will yield a different size and have different yarn requirements.

Notions
cable needle, waste yarn, extra needle same size or one size smaller than main needle

Stitches
For standard stitches, see page 128.

C6R-dec (cable 6 right with a decrease) — sl-3 sts to cable needle and hold to back, k2tog, k2, k3 from cable needle—1 st dec

C6R-inc (cable 6 right with an increase) — sl-3 sts to cable needle and hold to back, k3, p+k first st from cable needle, k2 from cable needle—1 st inc

Instructions

Scarf and shawl are worked flat. One strand of each yarn is held together throughout.

Instructions are given for scarf (shawl); when only one number is given, it applies to all sizes.

*Each pattern change is distinguished by a different repeat indicator for clarity: the cable edges are indicated by [...] and the diamond center is indicated by *{...}, repeat...*.*

cast on and setup

Cast on using tubular cast method, as follows: Using waste yarn, cast on 29 (67) sts and work 4 rows in stockinette (knit on right side, purl on wrong side), ending on WS row. Using main yarn (one strand of each yarn held together), work 3 rows in stockinette, ending on right side row.
With wrong side facing and using main yarn, *p1 from working needle, pick up and knit 1 from purl bump of first row of main yarn that is next to waste yarn,* repeat between * to last st, p1 — 57 (133) sts.

[chart on page 10]

Setup Row A (RS): *K1, p1,* repeat between * to last st, k1.
Setup Row B (WS): [P8, k1] 1 (3) times, {p4, k1} 7 (15) times, p4, [k1, p8] 1 (3) times.
Setup Row 1 (RS): [C8L, p1] 1 (3) times, *{C4R, p1} 4 times, {C4L, p1} 3 times, C4L,* p0 (p1), then repeat between * 0 (1) more time, [p1, C8R] 1 (3) times.

chart

Scarf is worked as 1-cable edge, 1 center section, 1-cable edge. Shawl is worked as 3-cable edge, 2 center sections, 3-cable edge. Refer to written instructions for setup of repeats and details of Rows S9 and F1.

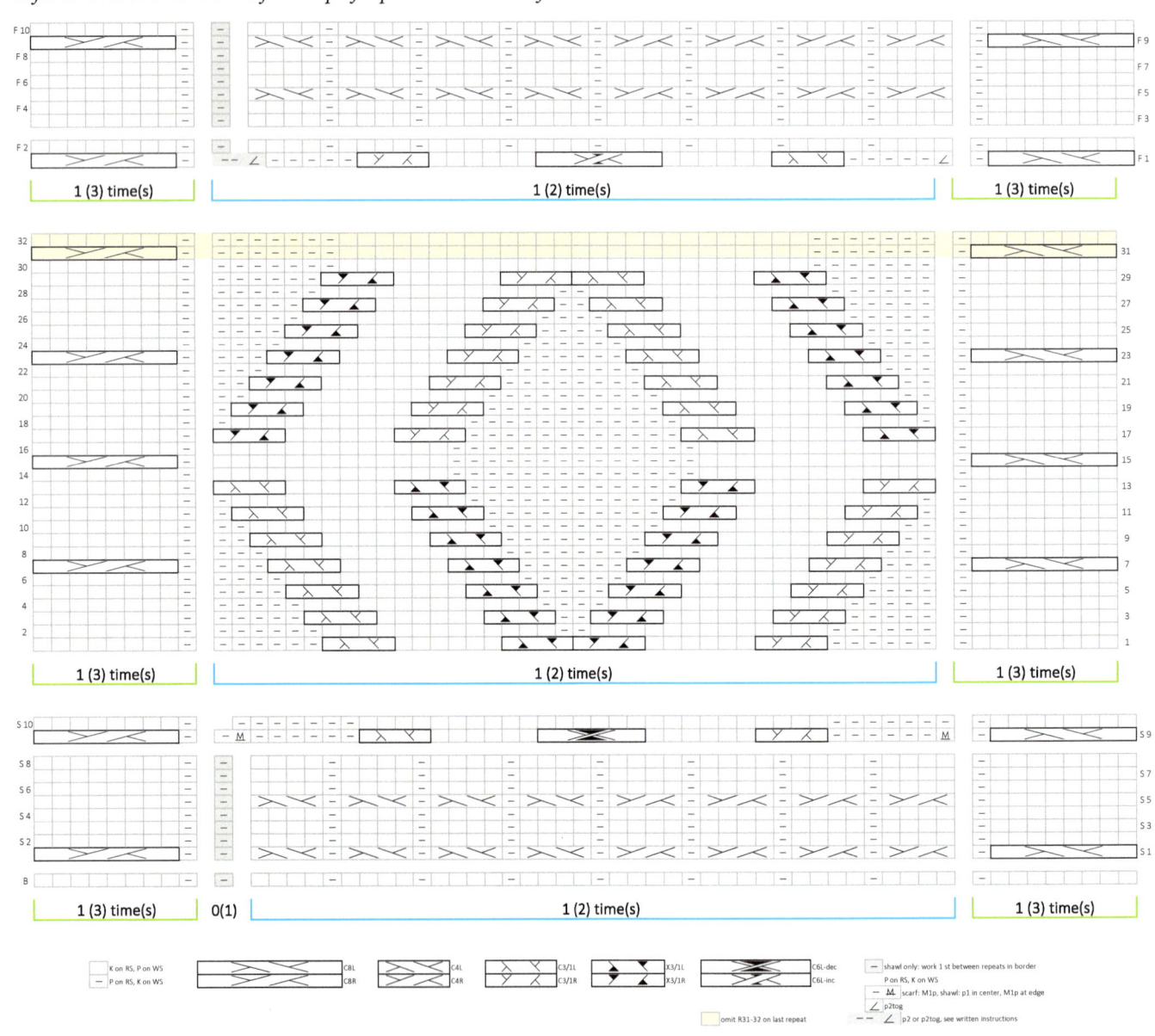

10

Setup Rows 2, 4, 6, 8 (WS): [P8, k1] 1 (3) times, {p4, k1} 7 (15) times, p4, [k1, p8] 1 (3) times.

Setup Row 3: [K8, p1] 1 (3) times, {k4, p1} 7 (15) times, k4, [p1, k8] 1 (3) times.

Setup Row 5: [K8, p1] 1 (3) times, *{C4R, p1} 4 times, {C4L, p1} 3 times, C4L,* p0 (p1), then repeat between * 0 (1) more time, [p1, k8] 1 (3) times.

Setup Row 7: Repeat Setup Row 3.

Repeat Setup Rows 1-8 four more times until piece measures 5½" or desired length, ending on Setup Row 8 — 42 rows total.

Setup Row 9 (scarf only): [C8L, p1] 1 time, M1p, p6, C3/1R, k6, C6R-dec, k6, C3/1L, p6, M1p, [p1, C8R] 1 time—1 st inc, 58 sts.

Setup Row 9 (shawl only): [C8L, p1] 3 times, M1p, p6, C3/1R, k6, C6R-dec, k6, C3/1L, p7, M1p, p6, C3/1R, k6, C6R-dec, k6, C3/1L, p6, M1p, [p1, C8R] 3 times — 1 st inc, 134 sts.

Setup Row 10 (all): [P8, k1] 1 (3) times, *k7, p26, k7,* repeat between * 0 (1) more time, [k1, p8] 1 (3) times — 58 (134) sts.

main section

[chart on page 10]

Row 1 (RS): [K8, p1] 1 (3) times, *p6, C3/1R, k6, X3/1R, X3/1L, k6, C3/1L, p6,* repeat between * 0 (1) more time, [p1, k8] 1 (3) times.

Row 2: [P8, k1] 1 (3) times, *k6, p13, k2, p13, k6,* repeat between * 0 (1) more time, [k1, p8] 1 (3) times.

Row 3: [K8, p1] 1 (3) times, *p5, C3/1R, k6, X3/1R, p2, X3/1L, k6, C3/1L, p5,* repeat between * 0 (1) more time, [p1, k8] 1 (3) times.
Row 4: [P8, k1] 1 (3) times, *k5, p13, k4, p13, k5,* repeat between * 0 (1) more time, [k1, p8] 1 (3) times.
Row 5: [K8, p1] 1 (3) times, *p4, C3/1R, k6, X3/1R, p4, X3/1L, k6, C3/1L, p4,* repeat between * 0 (1) more time, [p1, k8] 1 (3) times.
Row 6: [P8, k1] 1 (3) times, *k4, p13, k6, p13, k4,* repeat between * 0 (1) more time, [k1, p8] 1 (3) times.
Row 7: [C8L, p1] 1 (3) times, *p3, C3/1R, k6, X3/1R, p6, X3/1L, k6, C3/1L, p3,* repeat between * 0 (1) more time, [p1, C8R] 1 (3) times.
Row 8: [P8, k1] 1 (3) times, *k3, p13, k8, p13, k3,* repeat between * 0 (1) more time, [k1, p8] 1 (3) times.
Row 9: [K8, p1] 1 (3) times, *p2, C3/1R, k6, X3/1R, p8, X3/1L, k6, C3/1L, p2,* repeat between * 0 (1) more time, [p1, k8] 1 (3) times.
Row 10: [P8, k1] 1 (3) times, *k2, p13, k10, p13, k2,* repeat between * 0 (1) more time, [k1, p8] 1 (3) times.
Row 11: [K8, p1] 1 (3) times, *p1, C3/1R, k6, X3/1R, p10, X3/1L, k6, C3/1L, p1,* repeat between * 0 (1) more time, [p1, k8] 1 (3) times.
Row 12: [P8, k1] 1 (3) times, *k1, p13, k12, p13, k1,* repeat between * 0 (1) more time, [k1, p8] 1 (3) times.

Row 13: [K8, p1] 1 (3) times, *C3/1R, k6, X3/1R, p12, X3/1L, k6, C3/1L,* repeat between * 0 (1) more time, [p1, k8] 1 (3) times.
Row 14: [P8, k1] 1 (3) times, *p13, k14, p13,* repeat between * 0 (1) more time, [k1, p8] 1 (3) times.
Row 15: [C8L, p1] 1 (3) times, *k13, p14, k13,* repeat between * 0 (1) more time, [p1, C8R] 1 (3) times.
Row 16: [P8, k1] 1 (3) times, *p13, k14, p13,* repeat between * 0 (1) more time, [k1, p8] 1 (3) times.
Row 17: [K8, p1] 1 (3) times, *X3/1L, k6, C3/1L, p12, C3/1R, k6, X3/1R,* repeat between * 0 (1) more time, [p1, k8] 1 (3) times.
Row 18: [P8, k1] 1 (3) times, *k1, p13, k12, p13, k1,* repeat between * 0 (1) more time, [k1, p8] 1 (3) times.
Row 19: [K8, p1] 1 (3) times, *p1, X3/1L, k6, C3/1L, p10, C3/1R, k6, X3/1R, p1,* repeat between * 0 (1) more time, [p1, k8] 1 (3) times.
Row 20: [P8, k1] 1 (3) times, *k2, p13, k10, p13, k2,* repeat between * 0 (1) more time, [k1, p8] 1 (3) times.
Row 21: [K8, p1] 1 (3) times, *p2, X3/1L, k6, C3/1L, p8, C3/1R, k6, X3/1R, p2,* repeat between * 0 (1) more time, [p1, k8] 1 (3) times.
Row 22: [P8, k1] 1 (3) times, *k3, p13, k8, p13, k3,* repeat between * 0 (1) more time, [k1, p8] 1 (3) times.
Row 23: [C8L, p1] 1 (3) times, *p3, X3/1L, k6, C3/1L, p6, C3/1R, k6, X3/1R, p3,* repeat between * 0 (1) more time, [p1, C8R] 1 (3) times.
Row 24: [P8, k1] 1 (3) times, *k4, p13, k6, p13, k4,* repeat between * 0 (1) more time, [k1, p8] 1 (3) times.
Row 25: [K8, p1] 1 (3) times, *p4, X3/1L, k6, C3/1L, p4, C3/1R, k6, X3/1R, p4,* repeat between * 0 (1) more time, [p1, k8] 1 (3) times.
Row 26: [P8, k1] 1 (3) times, *k5, p13, k4, p13, k5,* repeat between * 0 (1) more time, [k1, p8] 1 (3) times.
Row 27: [K8, p1] 1 (3) times, *p5, X3/1L, k6, C3/1L, p2, C3/1R, k6, X3/1R, p5,* repeat between * 0 (1) more time, [p1, k8] 1 (3) times.
Row 28: [P8, k1] 1 (3) times, *k6, p13, k2, p13, k6,* repeat between * 0 (1) more time, [k1, p8] 1 (3) times.
Row 29: [K8, p1] 1 (3) times, *p6, X3/1L, k6, C3/1L, C3/1R, k6, X3/1R, p6,* repeat between * 0 (1) more time, [p1, k8] 1 (3) times.
Row 30: [P8, k1] 1 (3) times, *k7, p26, k7,* repeat between * 0 (1) more time, [k1, p8] 1 (3) times.
Row 31: [C8L, p1] 1 (3) times, *p7, k26, p7,* repeat between * 0 (1) more time, [p1, C8R] 1 (3) times.
Row 32: [P8, k1] 1 (3) times, *k7, p26, k7,* repeat between * 0 (1) more time, [k1, p8] 1 (3) times.

Repeat Main Section Rows 1-32: 10 (12) more times, then repeat Rows 1-30 again — 382 (446) rows in this section, 426 (490) rows total.

finishing and bind off

[chart on page 10]

Finish Row 1 (scarf only): [C8L, p1] 1 time, p2tog, p5, C3/1L, k6, C6R-inc, k6, C3/1R, p5, p2tog, [p1, C8R] 1 times — 1 st dec, 57 sts.
Finish Row 1 (shawl only): [C8L, p1] 3 times, p2tog, p5, C3/1L, k6, C6R-inc, k6, C3/1R, p5, p2tog, p7, C3/1L, k6, C6R-inc, k6, C3/1R, p5, p2tog, [p1, C8R] 3 times — 1 st dec, 133 sts.
Finish Rows 2, 4, 6, 8, 10: [P8, k1] 1 (3) times, *{{p4, k1}} 7 (15) times, p4,* repeat between * 0 (1) more time, [k1, p8] 1 (3) times.
Finish Row 3: [K8, p1] 1 (3) times, *{{k4, p1}} 7 (15) times, k4,* [p1, k8] 1 (3) times.
Finish Row 5: [K8, p1] 1 (3) times, *{C4R, p1} 4 times, {C4L, p1} 3 times, C4L,* p0 (p1), then repeat between * 0 (1) more time, [p1, k8] 1 (3) times.
Finish Row 7: [K8, p1] 1 (3) times, *{k4, p1} 7 (15) times, k4,* [p1, k8] 1 (3) times.
Finish Row 9: [C8L, p1] 1 (3) times, *{C4R, p1} 4 times, {C4L, p1} 3 times, C4L,* p0 (p1), then repeat between * 0 (1) more time, [p1, C8R] 1 (3) times.

Repeat Finish Rows 3-10 four more times until Finishing section measures same as Setup section, ending on Finish Row 10.

Bind off using tubular bind off as follows:

Bindoff Row A (RS): *K1, p1,* repeat between * to last st, k1.
Bindoff Row B (WS): *Sl-1 wyif, k1,* repeat between * to last st, sl-1 wyif.
Bindoff Row C (RS): *K1, sl-1 wyif,* repeat between * to last st, k1.

Separate front and back sts as follows: using extra needle held at back of work, *sl-1 to extra needle and hold to back of work, sl-1 to main needle and hold to front of work,* repeat between * to last st, sl-1 to extra needle. Using Kitchener stitch, graft front and back sts together.

Remove waste yarn from cast on.
Weave in ends. Block.

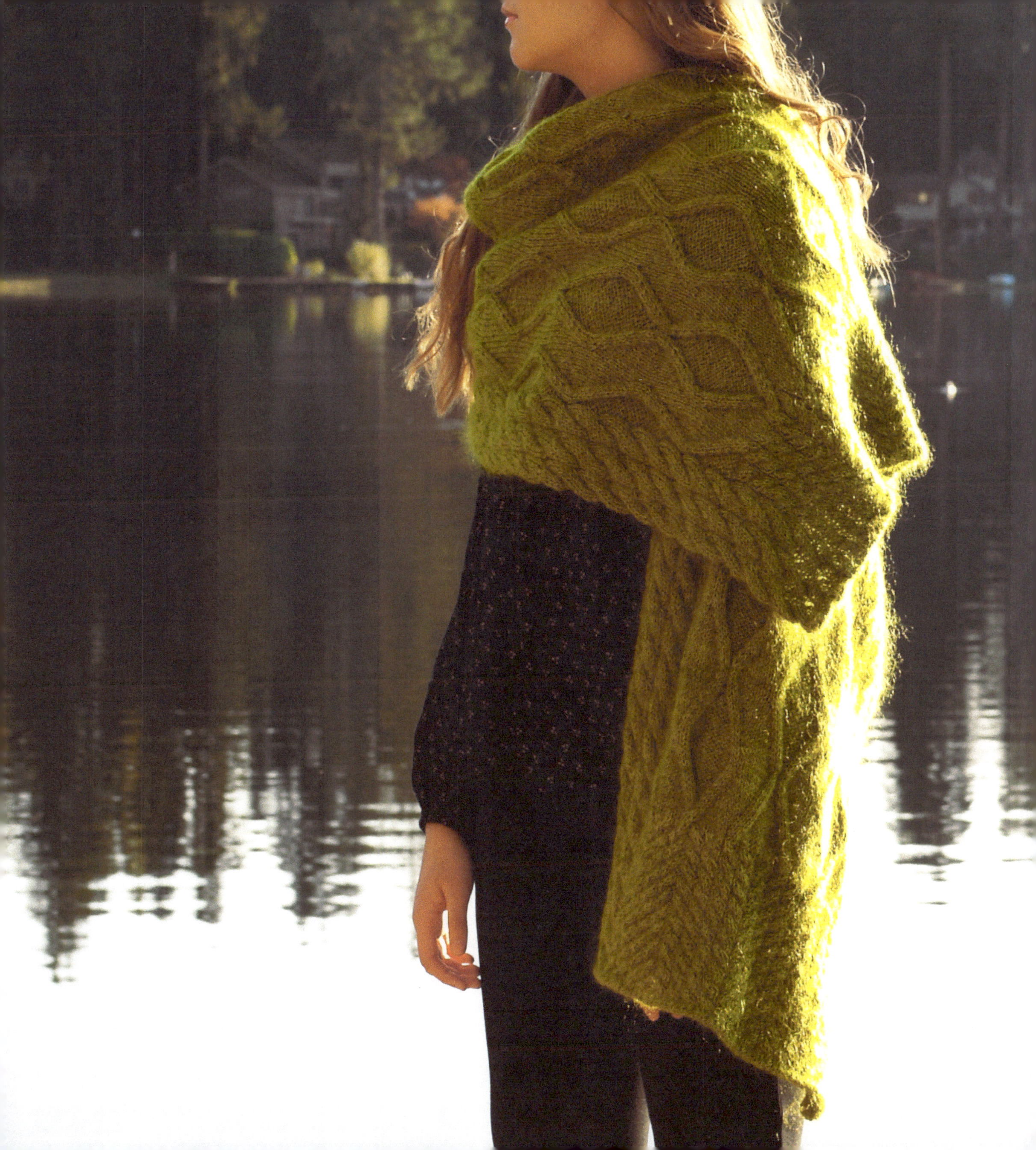

bespoke

on the menu

Brunch and bubbles. Bubbles and brunch. Either way they are an ideal combination.

Sweet, sour, butter, and bacon—the flavors of breakfast are all present in this wonderful brunch of sourdough Belgian waffles, French toast made from homemade orange zest raisin bread, crispy bacon, fresh blueberries, sweet and tangy balsamic peaches, and dark maple syrup. Crispy fluffy waffles, creamy French toast, and crunchy bacon—all of the textures of breakfast are here, too. But this is brunch, so of course there must be bubbles!

The Farmhouse Block Extra Brut Rosé from Full Pull Wines is simply gorgeous. Made from Marchant Vineyard Pinot Noir grapes using the traditional méthode champenoise, this delicious sparkling wine is slightly pink with small effervescent bubbles. The wine has aromas of fresh fruit, strawberries and cherries, flavors of ripe strawberries, a bit of Pinot Noir funkiness, a clean, crisp minerality and an almost bitter finish. This wine perfectly complements and contrasts with the flavors and textures of our brunch.

food

orange zest raisin bread (page 19)
Kevin's french toast (page 21)
fresh or balsamic peaches (page 21)
blueberries and orange slices
dark maple syrup
whipped cream (optional)
pepper bacon
freshly ground and brewed coffee
freshly squeezed orange juice

wine

Farmhouse Block Wines
NV Extra Brut Pinot Noir Rose
Marchant Vineyard

cooking & plating

1) For french toast, prepare bread up to 2 days in advance.

2) Prepare balsamic peaches up to 1 day in advance.

3) Squeeze the orange juice and make whipped cream. Refrigerate until ready to serve.

4) Wash berries, slice peaches, and peel and section oranges for topping or garnish, set aside. Cook bacon, set aside.

5) Start coffee brewing.

6) Make sourdough waffles or pancakes and french toast.

7) Serve food family style and allow everyone to serve themselves. Pour bubbles, coffee and orange juice at the table.

recipes

orange zest raisin bread/french toast
sourdough waffles (or pancakes)
balsamic peaches

orange zest raisin bread

Sourdough bread is made in 3 steps: proofing the starter and reserving some for later use, making the dough, then forming and baking the bread.

All measurements are by weight (this is important!).

Proof the starter
24 oz. sourdough starter
8 oz. water
8 oz. all-purpose flour

   1)   Combine all ingredients in a bowl and stir well. Let ferment 8-12 hours or overnight to proof.

There will be approximately 40 oz. of proofed sourdough. The sourdough is properly proofed when it is uniformly covered by small foamy-looking bubbles and has a delightfully sour aroma.

Make the dough
16 oz. proofed sourdough starter*
24 oz. all-purpose flour
10 oz. water
8 oz. raisins
2 oz. brown sugar
1 oz. orange zest, minced
½ oz. salt
¼ tsp. cinnamon
olive oil, if baking in pans

store the remaining 24 oz. starter from the proofing stage in a clean crock in the refrigerator for the next batch of bread

2) Combine all ingredients except the flour in a large bowl and mix thoroughly. Add the flour and knead into a ball of dough. Cover with plastic wrap or a cloth and let rise overnight or until doubled in volume.
For plain sourdough bread, omit the brown sugar, raisins, orange zest, and cinnamon.

3) After doubling, gently knead the dough into a ball. Use minimal flour if needed to keep the dough from sticking. Let rise until doubled, approximately 1-2 hours. Repeat this step one more time.

Form and bake the bread
4) Divide the dough in half, form into loaves, and place in lightly oiled bread pans or form into a desired shape. Cover with a cloth and let rise until doubled, approximately 1-2 hours.

About 30 minutes before dough has doubled, preheat oven to 425°F.

5) Just before baking, cut a slit into the tops of the loaves. Bake 20 minutes on bottom rack and then move to second-from-bottom rack for an additional 15-20 minutes until dark golden brown on top and the loaves make a hollow sound when tapped; total baking time is 35-40 minutes. Remove from the oven and place on a rack to cool. Wait 5 minutes before removing the loaves from bread pans. Allow bread to cool completely before using.

For plain sourdough bread, bake for a total of 30-35 minutes until dark golden brown on top and the loaves make a hollow sound when tapped.

Makes 2 loaves of bread.

balsamic peaches

4 fresh ripe peaches, thinly sliced
¼ c. dark balsamic vinegar
½ tsp. dried spearmint leaves, crushed

Combine peaches, balsamic vinegar, and mint in bowl. Cover and refrigerate overnight.

The mint must be dried; fresh mint will be too strongly flavored. Other mints would also work well.

Makes approximately 3 cups.

Kevin's french toast

4 eggs
¾ c. milk
1 Tbl. sugar
1 pinch salt
½ tsp. vanilla (optional)
3 Tbl. butter for cooking
8 slices orange zest raisin bread, ¾" thick

1) Combine eggs, milk, sugar, salt, and vanilla in a bowl. Whisk until combined. Pour mixture into a flat-bottomed dish large enough to hold two slices of bread.

2) Place a large skillet over medium to medium high heat. Add 1 Tbl. of butter. Melt the butter until it begins to foam. Evenly spread the melted butter around the skillet using a paper towel to season the pan.

3) While butter is melting, soak two bread slices in the egg and milk mixture for 30 seconds on each side.

4) Add ½ Tbl. butter to the hot pan, melting until it bubbles. Carefully place bread slices into the hot skillet. Keep the slices separated in the skillet so they do not stick together. Cook until nicely browned, 2-3 minutes on each side. Adjust heat as needed to prevent burning.

Makes 4 servings.

sourdough waffles or pancakes

For best results, measure ingredients by weight.

16 oz. proofed sourdough batter (3 c.)
6 oz. flour (1½ c.)
6 oz. water* (¾ c.)
6 oz. milk (¾ c.)
1 large egg, whisked until light and frothy
1½ oz. melted butter or vegetable oil (2 Tbl.)
1 oz. sugar (2 Tbl.)
½ oz. sea salt (2 tsp.)
¼ oz. baking soda (1 tsp.)

*For pancakes, reduce water to 4 oz. (½ c.)

1) Combine sugar, salt, and baking soda in a small bowl, mixing thoroughly to remove lumps. Set aside.

2) Combine the proofed sourdough batter, flour, water, milk, egg, and butter or vegetable oil. Whisk gently to just combine, 30-40 seconds. Streaks of the melted butter or vegetable oil are OK here; it will be whisked again later.

3) Add the sugar, salt, and baking soda mixture to the batter and whisk to thoroughly combine all ingredients, 30-40 seconds or until all of the butter or oil is mixed into the batter with no streaks.

4) Let the batter rest 2-3 minutes.

5) Make waffles following the instructions for your waffle maker, or make pancakes.

Makes approximately 8 Belgian waffles, 12-15 regular waffles, or a whole bunch of pancakes.

Sourdough waffles and pancakes are also delicious topped with citrus caramel pears (see page 123).

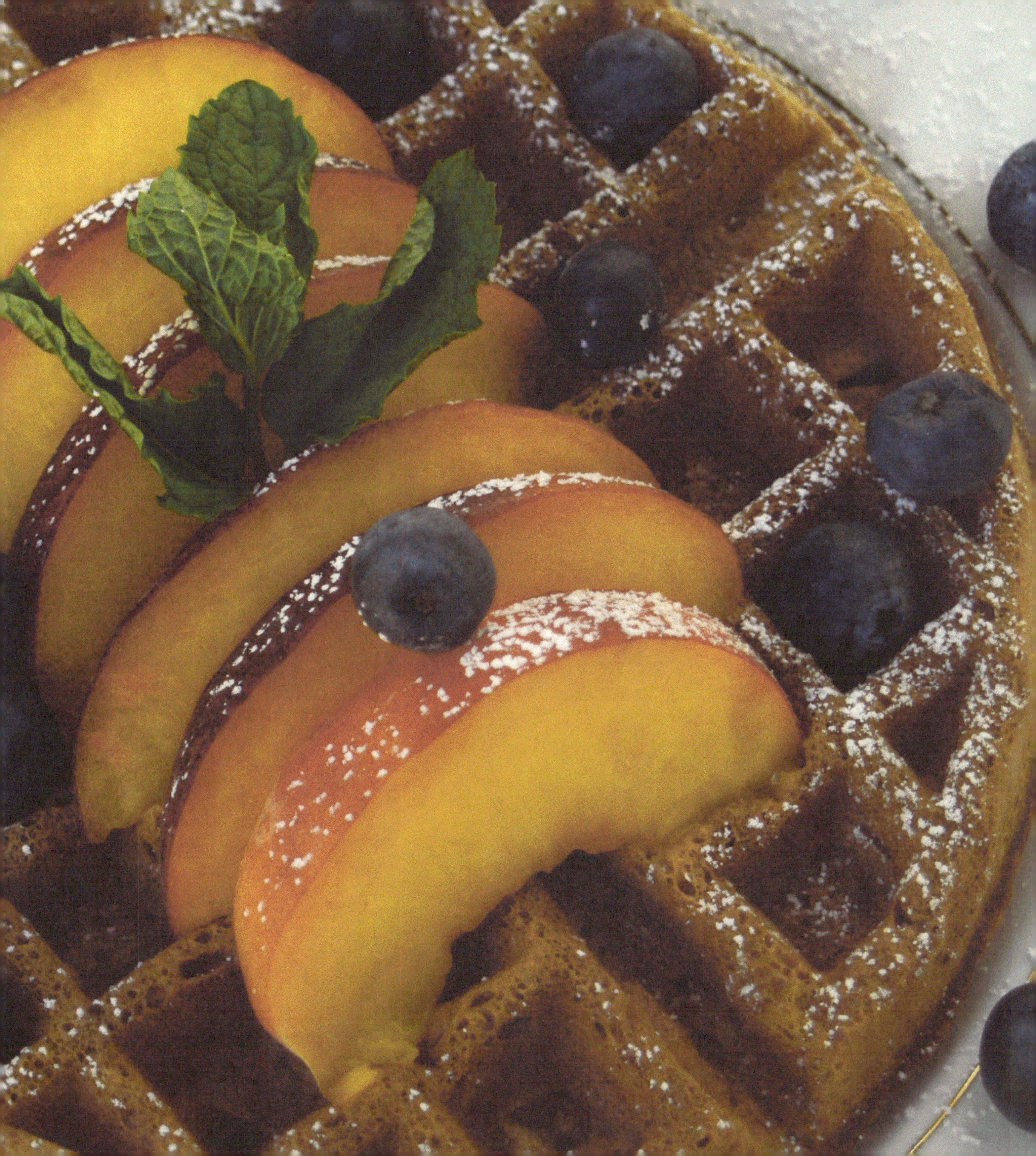

in the newwool dyed

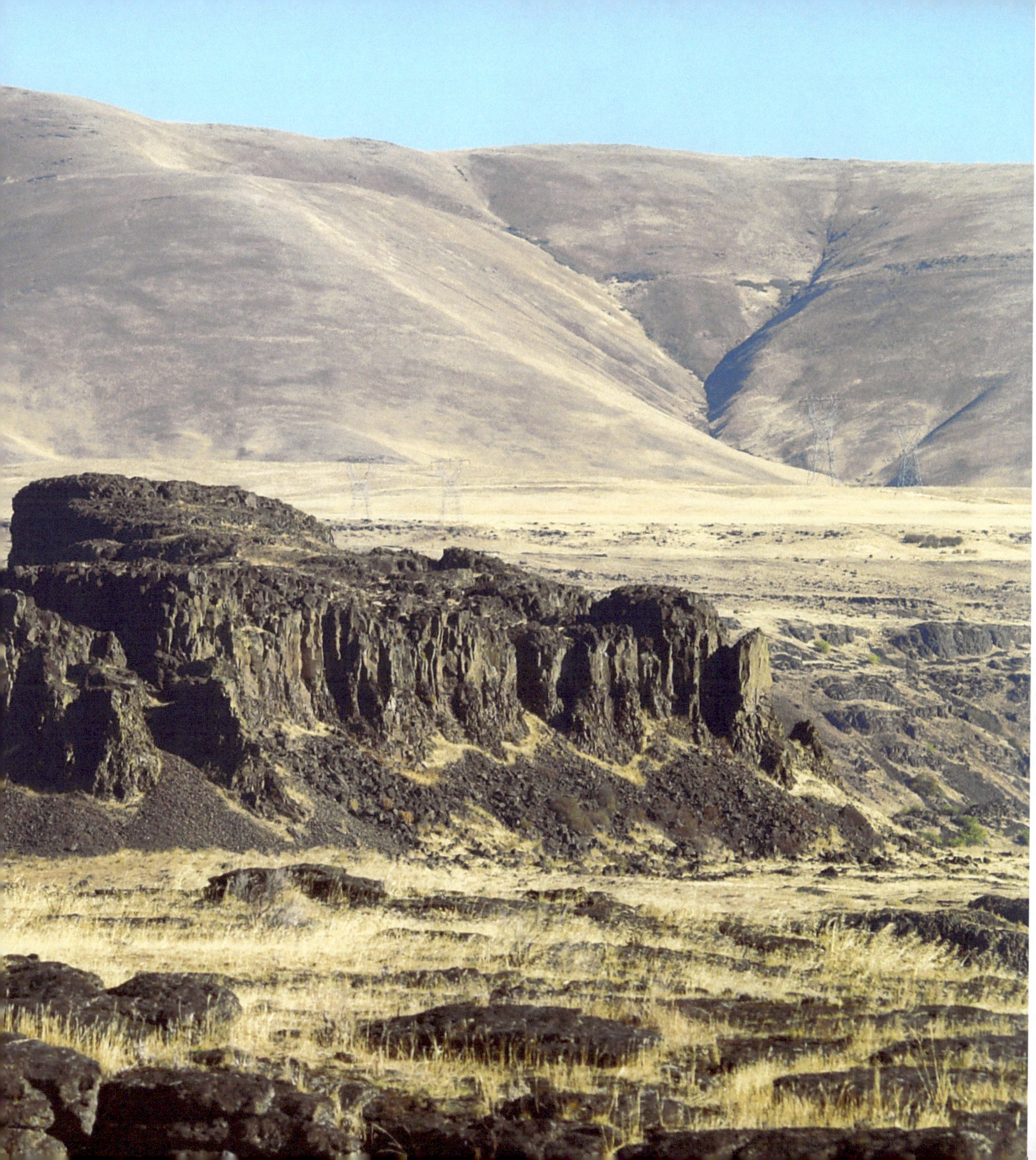

"Dyed in the wool" — the phrase evokes deep rich color and texture like no other. Unique. Special. Whether making stunning yarns or gorgeous wines, beauty begins at the source using the highest quality raw materials.

on pins & needles

Unusual fiber blends and deep layers of color signal the work of The Homestead Hobbyist Kenneth Moore.

Ken carefully selects and combines fibers with textures and colors that will tantalize knitters (and spinners).

His gorgeous yarn lines start with a special or unusual breed like Polwarth, Criolla, Shetland, Rambouillet, Merino,

CVM/Romeldale, Camel, or Alpaca. Some of his yarns even add a splash of Mulberry or Tussah Silk.

The fibers are cleaned and dyed—sometimes all one color, sometimes many colors—and then blended during carding, combing, or other pre-spinning processing for extra rich and deep color.

During spinning and plying at small or local mills, the saturated colors meld and become more subtle. The end result is a beautiful, layered, meticulously crafted, small batch fiber or yarn that is sheer bliss to spin or knit or weave and is wonderful to wear.

on the menu

Creamy, round, chalky, smooth, dusty, silky, full, watery, soft, rough, velvety—it is amazing how much of an impact that texture, also known as mouthfeel, has on the enjoyment of wine. Hillary Sjolund of Sonoris Wines takes her texture seriously.

She began her career in wine performing analytical chemistry on grapes and wine, deepened her love of the culture of wine during harvest in Chile, and honed her winemaking skills at California and Washington wineries before founding Enomama, her wine analysis laboratory, and Sonoris Wines in 2011.

Hillary's combination of a scientific mind and creative spirit along with her mastery of sensory perception allows her to produce wines with incredible textures, flavors, and aromas—wines that are technically balanced and uniquely expressive. In addition to wine production and chemistry, Hillary also teaches wine education courses including a wine aroma workshop that was fun, challenging and informative—it was one of our favorite wine-related experiences.

Family, friends, good food, good wine, and learning a bit along the way—it sounds perfect to us!

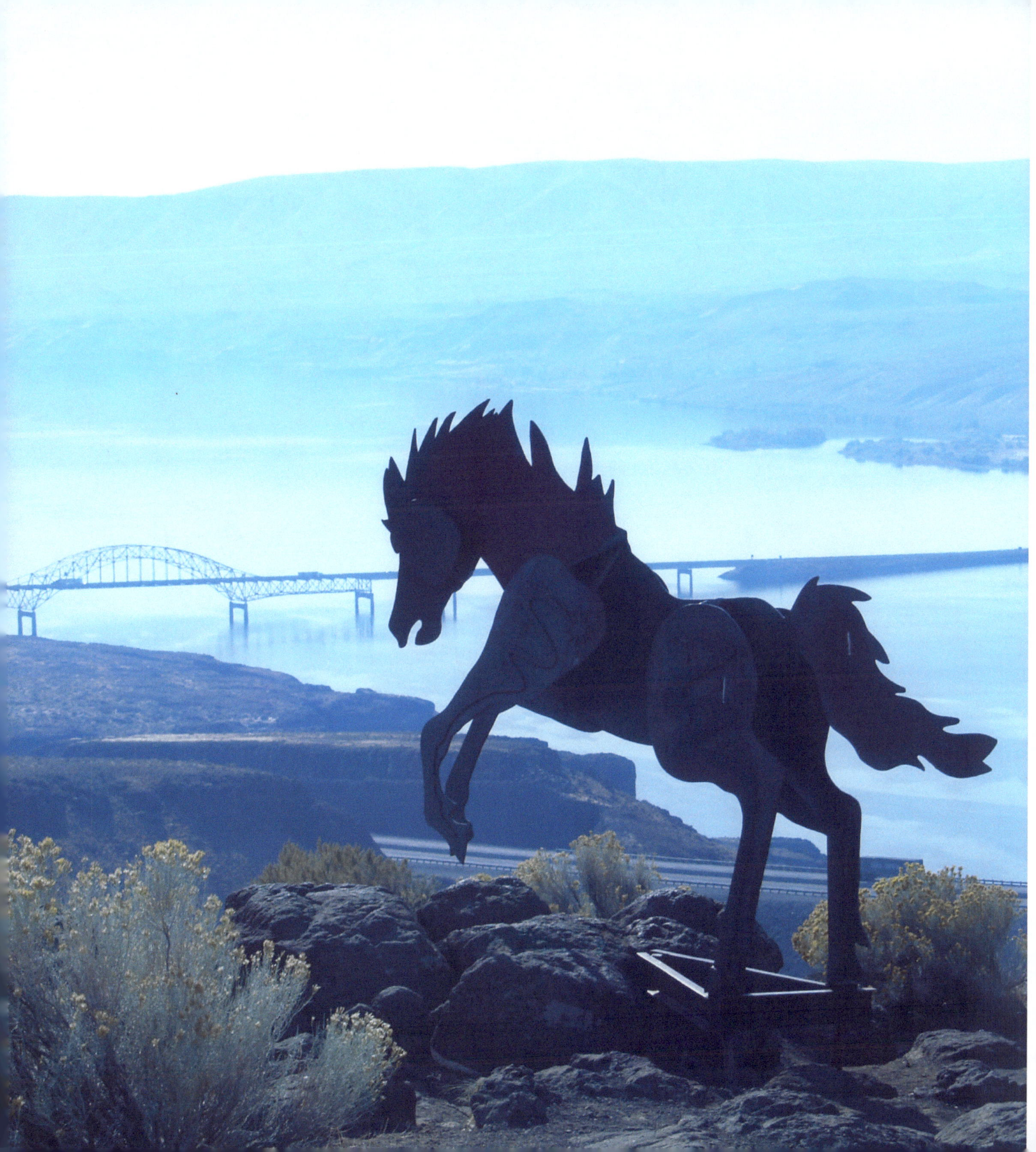

hand dyed the wood

on pins & needles

Cold feet on a chilly afternoon were the inspiration for these snuggly warm lounge socks.

The simple ribbing lets the beauty of the yarn shine through, an interesting stripe series based on the Fibonacci Sequence allows for a great range of fiber and color play, and sport weight yarn makes for a fairly quick knit of these charming socks.

Hand-spun yarn using beautiful or rare fibers would be a wonderful treat. Make identical or "fraternal twin" socks to suit the knitter's or recipient's mood. Mix and match favorite colors or fibers or textures for a truly unique creation.

fibonacci lounge socks

Size
S (M, L, XL, 2X) stretches to fit foot circumference of 6½" (8", 9¼", 10½", 12") / 16 (20, 23, 26, 30) cm

Yarn
Light DK weight (275 yds/100 g), 2 skeins (1 skein each of 2 colors)

Shown in Homestead Hobbyist Crime Scene DK: size M in Bloodstain (c1) + Tire Tracks (c2), size L in Tire Tracks (c1) + Deputy (c2).

Gauge and Needles
24 sts & 32 rows = 4"/10 cm in stockinette, 34 sts & 32 rows = 4"/10 cm in relaxed 2x2 ribbing (easily stretches to same gauge as stockinette), both using US 3-5 (3.25-3.75mm) or size needed to get gauge.

For proper fit, take time to check gauge.

Notions
stitch markers, waste yarn

Stitches
For standard stitches, see page 128.

c1, c2 — color 1, color 2

Instructions

Socks are worked in the round from the top down with an afterthought heel.

Socks are identical, make 2.

Cuff and leg
Using c1, cast on 40 (48, 56, 64, 72) sts. Join to knit in the round, being careful not to twist. PM for end of round.

Pattern Round: *K2, p2,* repeat between * around.

Work Pattern Round for number of rounds specified in Color Order list (see pg 34), switching colors as indicated. Cut ends for long floats of 5 or more rounds; carry yarn loosely up inside for floats of 3 or fewer rounds.

To place waste yarn for heel (see photo page 34, waste yarn = orange): Sl-1, using waste yarn k20 (24, 28, 32, 36), break waste yarn, slip 21 (25, 29, 33, 37) stitches back onto left needle.

Resume knitting with c1 in the round, continuing in established Pattern Round for the number of rounds specified in Color Order list until the entire list has been worked.

If custom length is desired, add or remove rounds in the final *"21 rounds in c2"* section.

Break c2.

Color Order

21 rounds in c1
1 round in c2
13 rounds in c1
1 round in c2
8 rounds in c1
2 rounds in c2
5 rounds in c1
3 rounds in c2
3 rounds in c1
5 rounds in c2
1 round in c1
—place waste yarn for heel—
1 round in c1
8 rounds in c2
1 round in c1
13 rounds in c2
1 round in c1
21 rounds in c2

Place waste yarn.

Unpick waste yarn, place sts on needles.

Toe
Setup: *Join c1.* Remove end of round marker, k1 with c1. PM for new end of round. Place another marker halfway around, so that there are 20 (24, 28, 32, 36) sts between each marker.

Round 1: *K2, work in established pattern to 2 sts before m, k2,* repeat between * again.
Round 2: *K1, ssk, work in established pattern to 3 sts before m, k2tog, k1,* repeat between * again.

Repeat Toe Rounds 1-2 until 16 sts remain.

Divide sts onto 2 needles with 8 sts on each needle. Graft together using Kitchener stitch.

Heel
Unpick waste yarn and place sts on needles — 40 (48, 56, 64, 72) sts (see photo page 34).

Join to knit in the round, being careful not to twist. PM for end of round. Place another marker halfway around, so that there are 20 (24, 28, 32, 36) sts between each marker.

Round 1: Knit.
Round 2: *K1, ssk, k to 3 sts before m, k2tog, k1,* repeat between * again.

Repeat Heel Rounds 1-2 until 16 sts remain.

Divide sts onto 2 needles with 8 sts on each needle. Graft together using Kitchener stitch.

Weave in ends. Hand wash. Dry flat.

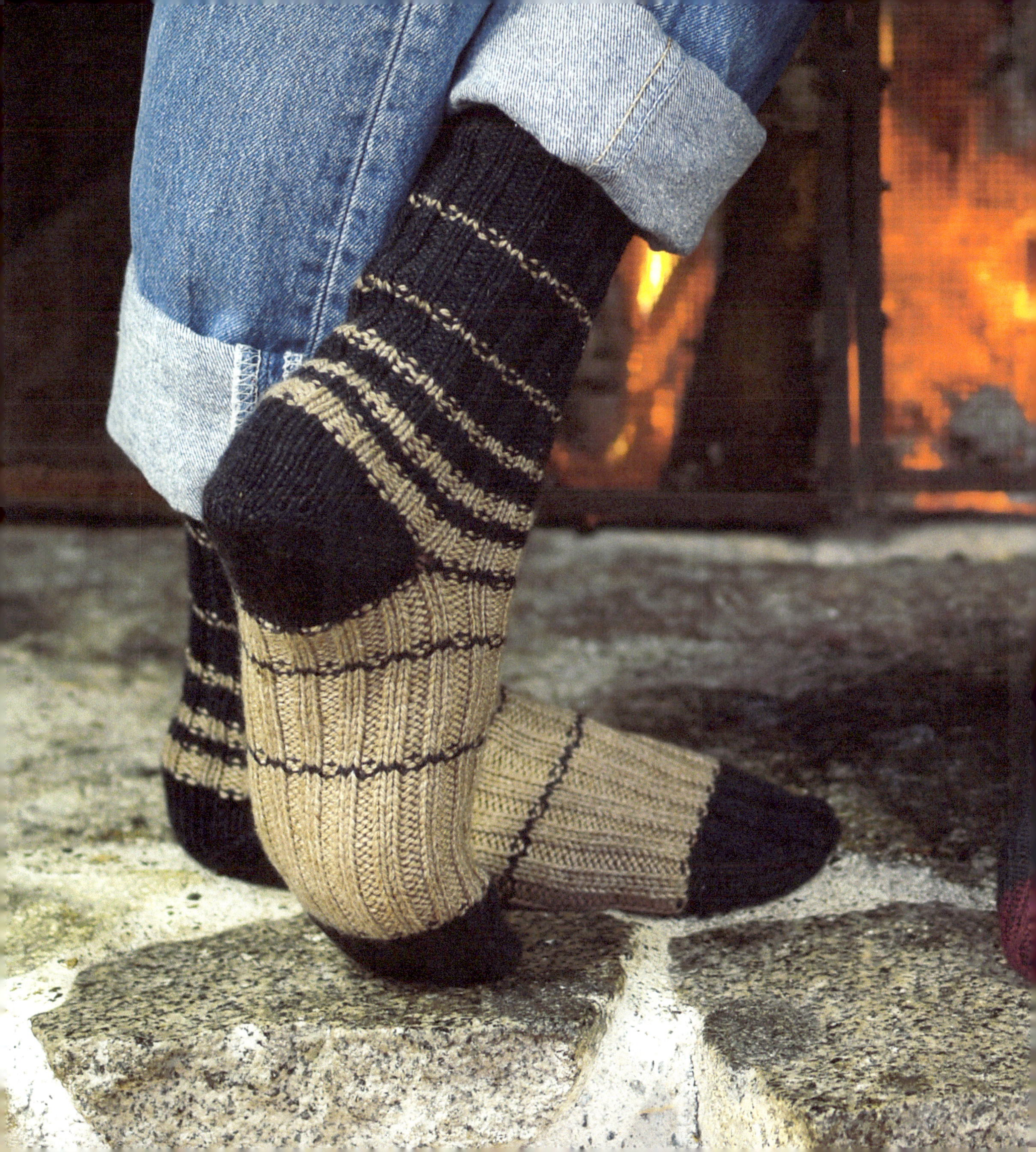

in the newwood aged

on the menu

On a blustery, rainy day—fairly common in the Pacific Northwest—there is nothing better than grilled sandwiches and soup by a roaring fire. With wine, of course!

In addition to the classic grilled cheddar, consider tomato + mozzarella, ham + gruyère or swiss, and for the more adventurous: prosciutto + provolone with arugula + honey. Made with homemade sourdough bread and grilled to crispy, melty perfection, these sandwiches are ready to be dunked. Our carrot-apple-ginger soup adds a bit of sophistication to this casual lunch and is excellent whether you decide to dunk or not.

The Sonoris Wines 2012 Verna Mae Viognier crisply highlights the flavors in the soup and cleanly pairs with the sandwiches. With aromas of apple, pear, honey, hay and pie spices and flavors of apple pie, vanilla, and a hint of lemon zest, the creaminess, well-balanced acidity, and clean mineral finish provide a refreshing complement to our soup and sandwiches.

The 2010 The Source Merlot offers an intense counterpoint for the meal. The aromas of raspberry, cherry, blueberry, vanilla and tobacco and the flavors of cherry, cedar, chocolate and dried herbs, along with the elegant tannins allow this wine to provide a rich contrast to the soup and sandwiches.

food

carrot-apple-ginger soup (page 39)
grilled sandwiches (page 40)
sourdough bread (page 19)
crispy bacon bits
goat cheese
chopped basil
olive oil
black lava salt

wine

Sonoris Wines
2010 The Source Merlot
2012 Verna Mae Viognier

cooking & plating

1)   Make soup up to 1 day in advance. Reheat soup starting about ½-hour before serving.

2)   Make grilled sandwiches. Cut in half or quarters, if desired.

3)   Arrange soup in bowls and garnish with crispy bacon bits, crumbled goat cheese, chopped basil, a drizzle of olive oil, or black lava salt, as desired.

4)   Plate sandwiches family style or individually—mix or match, as desired.

recipes

carrot-apple-ginger soup
grilled sandwiches
sourdough bread (page 19)

carrot-apple-ginger soup

1½-2 lbs. carrots, washed, peeled, coarsely chopped (6-8 large or 8-10 medium)
1-2 lbs. Granny Smith apples, peeled, cored, and chopped (2-3 apples)
1-1½ lbs. sweet onion, coarsely chopped (1 medium onion)
3-4 cloves garlic, peeled and chopped
½"-1" fresh ginger, peeled and minced
⅛ tsp. ground cayenne pepper
½ tsp. cinnamon
1 tsp. sea salt
1 tsp. freshly ground black pepper
1-2 Tbl. olive oil
3-4 c. water

1) Place olive oil in a stock pot over medium-high heat. Add all remaining ingredients except water to the pot and cook covered until carrots are tender, approximately 20-30 minutes, stirring occasionally.

2) Stir in 3 cups water.

39

3) Using an immersion blender, blend until smooth. Or, working in small batches, carefully pour ingredients into a food processor or blender and blend until smooth, then return soup to pot. Be careful when blending, soup is hot! Add more water, if needed, for desired consistency.

4) Simmer covered for 15 more minutes, stirring occasionally. Serve immediately or let cool, refrigerate, or freeze.

Makes approximately 3 quarts, 10-12 servings.

grilled sandwiches

8 slices hearty sandwich bread, ½" thick (plain sourdough bread, page 19, is tasty)
4 Tbl. softened butter
2 oz. each cheddar, mozzarella, gruyère or swiss, and provolone cheese, sliced or grated
2 oz. ham sliced thin
1 oz. prosciutto
1 tomato, sliced thin
¼ c. arugula, loosely packed
1 ripe pear, thinly sliced
1 Tbl. butter to melt in the pan
Dijon mustard (optional)
honey

1) Butter one side of each piece of bread using ½ Tbl. of softened butter.

2) Place a skillet large enough to hold one or more sandwiches over medium high heat. Add 1 Tbl. of butter and melt the butter until it begins to foam, approximately 1 minute. Swirl the butter to coat the bottom of the skillet and reduce heat to medium.

3) Build the sandwiches in the skillet one at a time by placing the first slice of bread in the skillet butter side down, layer on the ingredients, then place the second slice of bread on top, butter side up.

Sandwich option: straight up cheddar with a dab of mustard, if desired
Sandwich option: tomato and mozzarella
Sandwich option: arugula, prosciutto, pear, and provolone, with a drizzle of honey
Sandwich option: ham and gruyère or swiss with a dab of mustard, if desired

Change sandwich ingredients as desired.

4) Cook the sandwiches until nicely browned, 2-3 minutes, then flip and brown the other side. Add a small amount of additional butter for the second side if desired. Reduce the heat if necessary to prevent burning.

Makes 4 sandwiches.

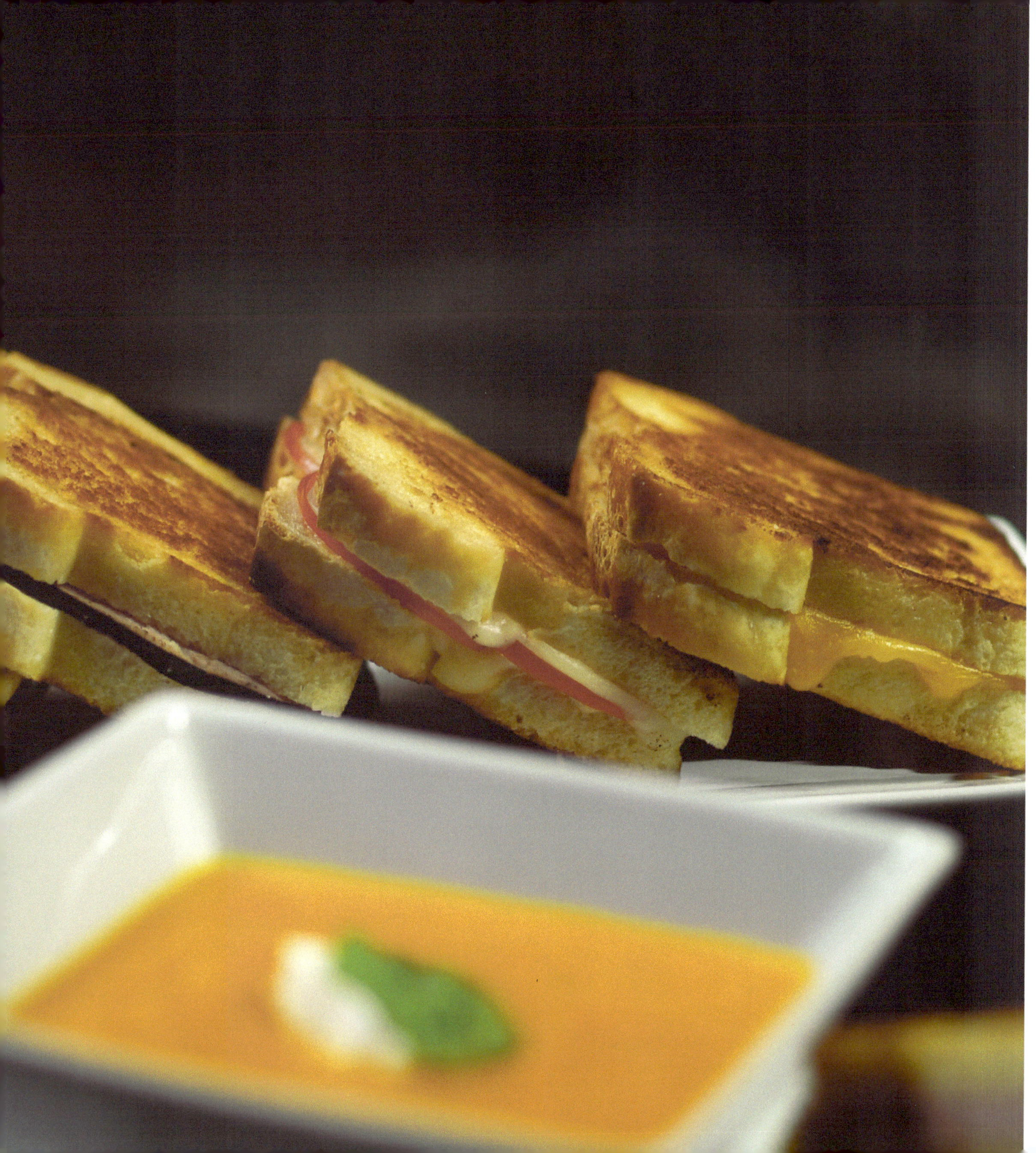

wild

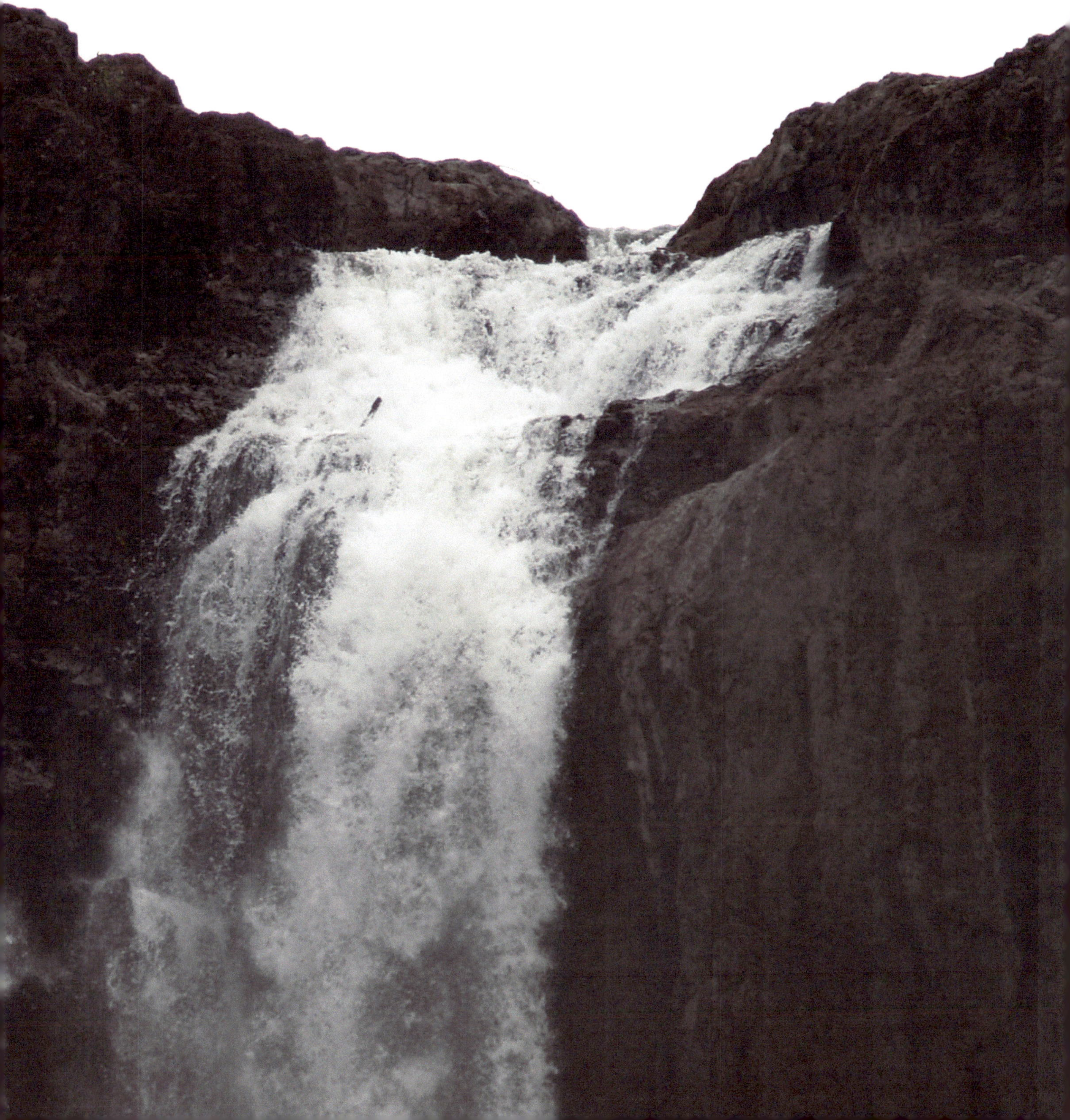

Start with passion, perserverence and hard work; add a generous helping of fun and interesting experiences; then combine it with a smart, driven woman and this is what you get…

on pins & needles

The notion of *grist creative* grew out of a love of yarn and wool and craft mingled with the desire to combine the bounty of locally-produced, family-owned businesses with my love of design.

The beauty of nature—the wildness of a waterfall, the call of a bird, a riot of colors in a field of flowers—inspires the designs and yarns of *grist creative*.

Like many of us, Mom taught me to knit, crochet, and sew at a young age.

Over the years, I learned about design and production, had a career in software development, and then came full circle back to my early love of craft.

"She tripped over a sheep and fell into a business," is how my husband describes my current adventure. It started with the publication of those first few patterns; moved into the design of a yarn and fiber line, more patterns and my first book **Black Sheep Creamery Knits**; followed by the publication of more patterns (always!) and more fun collaborations with yarnies that led to my second book **Northwest knits + eats** which generated so many ideas and interesting experiences that they bubbled over into this book. And here we are!

on the menu

Not all Damsels are in distress. Many—like Mari Womack, a.k.a. The Damsel of Damsel Cellars—are smart, passionate, hard-working women that have a dream and make it happen.

Mari got her training to make wine in the traditional way—she apprenticed with a master. Striking a deal in 2011 to manage the Darby Cellars tasting rooms in exchange for winemaking lessons, Mari's love of wine expanded into a passion for production and her nascent winery was born with her first two barrels of Syrah, her favorite varietal. Damsel Cellars has since expanded to embrace several fan favorites including Malbec, Cabernet Sauvignon, and two gorgeous blends: a GSM and a Bordeaux-style.

Mari's love of Syrah stems from its potential for endless variation that can be influenced by terroir, process, and winemaker preferences. It is well-suited for improvisational winemaking with many options depending on the style and vision of the winemaker—it can be fermented whole cluster, de-stemmed and crushed, stems can be added back to the fermenter, and it can be co-fermented with other varietals. Washington State Syrah tends to be fruit forward with a spicy kick and a peppery finish; dark, lush, full-bodied, and sometimes funky. It is wonderful paired with food, or simply savored on its own.

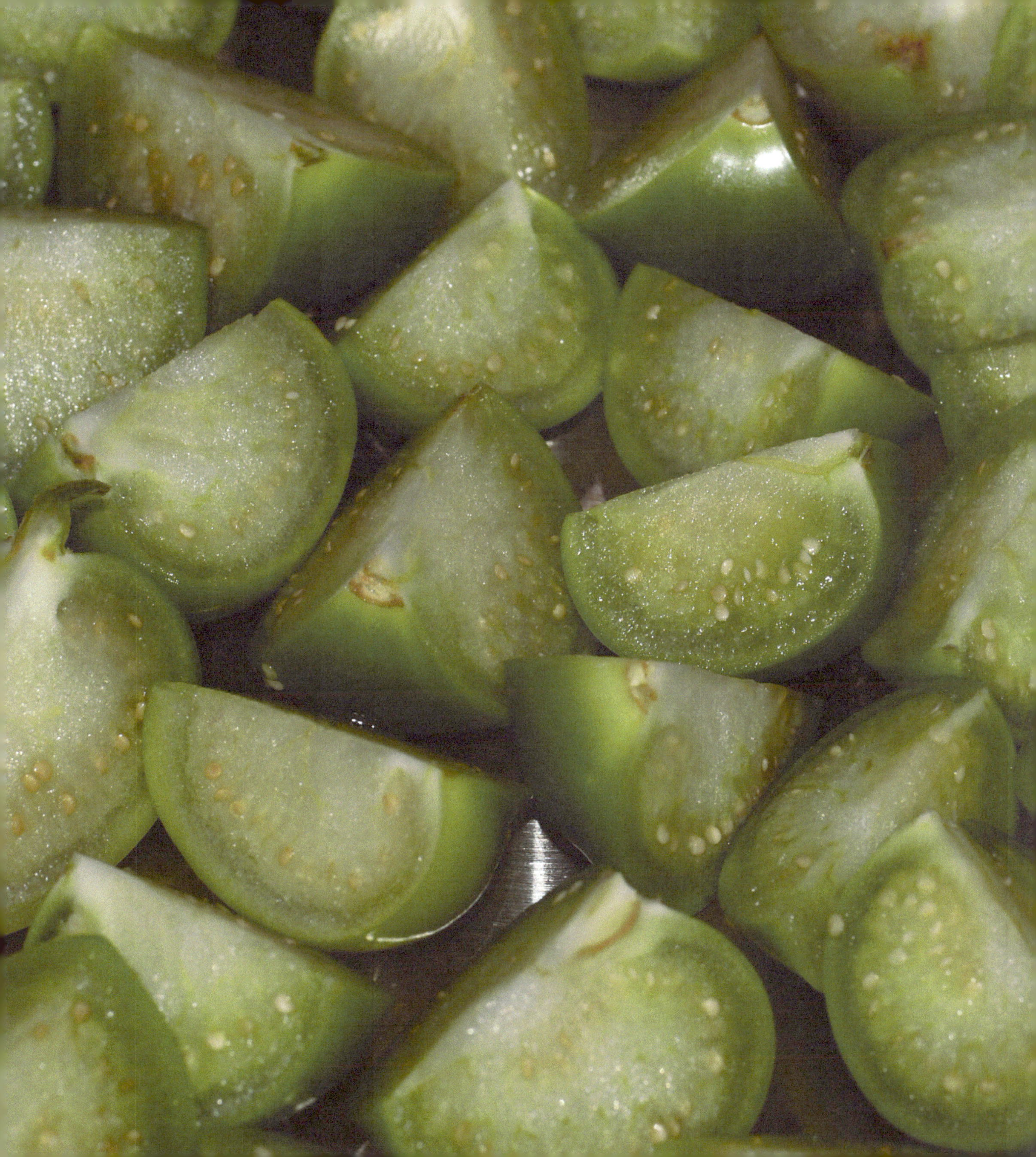

wild

on pins & needles

Water is one of the most prominent features of the Pacific Northwest—ocean, sound, lakes, rivers, and waterfalls define the landscape. Water for every season. Water for lush greenery. Water as energy. Water for inspiration. By mid-Spring, the snow in the mountains is melting and filling the raging rivers and breathtakingly beautiful waterfalls. Inspiration abounds.

This lace pattern began as a fragment of a stitch in a stitch dictionary. After numerous swatches of various repeats and offsets, I finally hit upon a simple flip with ongoing repeats and knew I had found just the thing to represent the flowing, churning, babbling, and rambling of water.

The springy Targhee wool yarn with ample twist gives great stitch definition for this motif that tumbles along the length of the scarf and cowl just like the swelling Snoqualmie Falls and River.

maverick

Size
Cowl: 20" wide x 43" circumference (50 x 110 cm)
Scarf: 11" wide x 80" long (28 x 200 cm)

Yarn
DK weight (238 yds/100 g), 700 yds

Shown in grist creative maverick, a limited edition 100% targhee wool yarn that is grown, spun and hand-dyed in the Pacific Northwest. Scarf shown in natural white and cowl shown in hand-dyed natural indigo, 3 skeins each.

Gauge and Needles
20 sts and 26 rows = 4" / 10 cm in pattern after blocking using US 6-8 (4-5mm) or size needed to get gauge.

Gauge is not critical for this project; a different gauge will yield a different size and have different yarn requirements.

Notions
waste yarn, crochet hook (for provisional cast on), extra needle in same size (for scarf tubular bind off)

Stitches
For standard stitches, see page 128.

Instructions

Cowl and scarf are both worked flat. Cowl starts with a provisional cast on, is worked flat, and then the ends are grafted together. Scarf starts with a tubular cast on and finishes with a tubular bind off.

Cowl cast on
Provisionally cast on 103 sts.

Scarf cast on
Using waste yarn, start tubular cast on by casting on on 28 sts. Still using waste yarn, work a few rows in stockinette, ending on WS (purl) row. Break waste yarn.
Scarf cast on Row 1 (RS): Using working yarn, knit.
Scarf cast on Row 2 (WS): Purl.
Scarf cast on Rows 3 (RS): Knit.
Join cast on into tube: With wrong side facing, p1 from working needle, *pick up and k1 from the lowest row of main yarn (the stitch looks like a purl bump), p1 from working needle,* repeat between * to end — 55 sts. Remove waste yarn.

cowl + scarf main section

For corded edging, stitches are slipped with yarn always on wrong side—this means if right side is facing, the stitch is slipped with yarn in back; and if wrong side is facing, the stitch is slipped with yarn in front. Snugly pull first stitch of each row to ensure corded edging wraps neatly.

Setup Row (WS): P3, *k1, p5,* repeat between * to last 4 sts, k1, p3.

maverick pattern

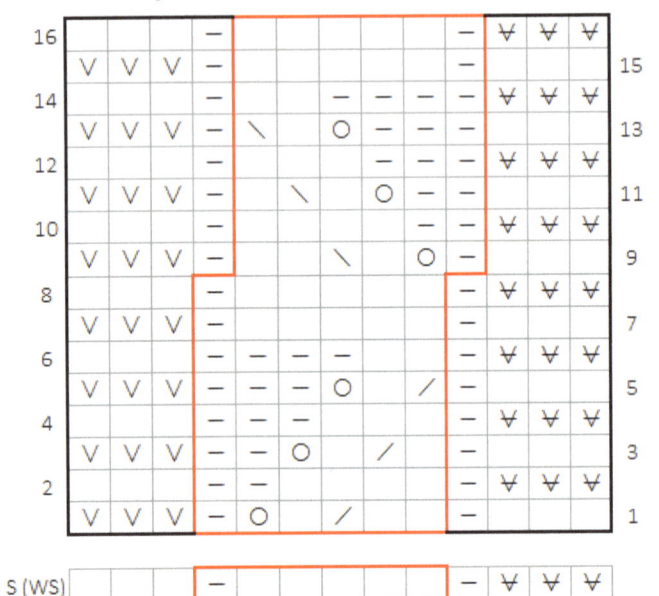

Legend:
- blank = K on RS, P on WS
- — = P on RS, K on WS
- V = slip with yarn in back (yarn on ws)
- ⋎ = slip with yarn in front (yarn on ws)
- / = k2tog
- \ = ssk
- O = yo

Row 1 (RS): K3, p1, *k2, k2tog, k1, yo, p1,* repeat bet * to last 3 sts, sl-3 wyib.
Row 2 (WS): P3, *k2, p4,* repeat between * to last 4 sts, k1, sl-3 wyif.
Row 3: K3, p1, *k1, k2tog, k1, yo, p2,* repeat between * to last 3 sts, sl-3 wyib.
Row 4: P3, *k3, p3,* repeat between * to last 4 sts, k1, sl-3 wyif.
Row 5: K3, p1, *k2tog, k1, yo, p3,* repeat between * to last 3 sts, sl-3 wyib.
Row 6: P3, *k4, p2,* repeat between * to last 4 sts, k1, sl-3 wyif.
Row 7: K3, p1, *k5, p1,* repeat between * to last 3 sts, sl-3 wyib.
Row 8: P3, *k1, p5,* repeat between * to last 4 sts, k1, sl-3 wyif.
Row 9: K3, *p1, yo, k1, ssk, k2,* repeat between * to last 4 sts, p1, sl-3 wyib.
Row 10: P3, k1, *p4, k2,* repeat between * to last 3 sts, sl-3 wyif.
Row 11: K3, *p2, yo, k1, ssk, k1,* repeat between * to last 4 sts, p1, sl-3 wyib.
Row 12: P3, k1, *p3, k3,* repeat between * to last 3 sts, sl-3 wyif.
Row 13: K3, *p3, yo, k1, ssk,* repeat between * to last 4 sts, p1, sl-3 wyib.
Row 14: P3, k1, *p2, k4,* repeat between * to last 3 sts, sl-3 wyif.
Row 15: K3, *p1, k5,* repeat between * to last 4 sts, p1, sl-3 wyib.
Row 16: P3, k1, *p5, k1,* repeat between * to last 3 sts, sl-3 wyif.

Repeat Rows 1-16 until piece measures 43" for cowl or 80" for scarf or desired length, ending on Row 15 for cowl or Row 16 for scarf. For bind off and finishing, keep at least 3 yards of yarn remaining for cowl and at least 3 yards plus 4 rows of yarn remaining for scarf.

bind off and finishing

Cowl is grafted together into a loop and scarf is finished with a tubular bind off to match cast on.

Cowl bind off
Unpick provisional cast on and place sts on extra needle. Join to form a loop, being careful not to twist. Graft first and last rows together using Kitchener stitch.
Weave in ends. Hand wash. Dry flat.

Scarf bind off
Bind off Row 1 (RS): K1, *p1, k1,* repeat between * to end.
Bind off Row 2 (WS): Sl-1 wyif, *k1, sl-1 wyif,* repeat between * to end.
Bind off Row 3 (RS): K1, *sl-1 wyif, k1,* repeat between * to end.
Divide stitches onto two needles: Hold extra needle toward back of work, sl-1 to extra needle, *sl-1 to working needle, sl-1 to extra needle,* repeat between * to end. Graft stitches together using Kitchener stitch.
Weave in ends. Hand wash. Dry flat.

wild
Damsel
CELLARS
2015
BOUSHEY VINEYARD
YAKIMA VALLEY
CABERNET FRANC
Damsel
CELLARS
STILLWATER CREEK
VINEYARD
SYRAH

on the menu

This pairing was easy! When asked about favorite foods, The Damsel herself, Mari Womack, replied "mole!" every time. So, mole it is.

This dish is based on a fairly traditional mole negro with a twist: the addition of the aji mirasol dried chili pepper from Peru. This chili pepper adds a medium heat and flavors and aromas of apricot and citrus, dried orange and lemon zest. The flavors of braised pork slow-roasted with cumin and coriander deepen when combined with the mole to make the empanada filling. Served on a base of queso blanco béchamel sauce, decorated with oregano and jalapeño oils, and garnished with fresh jalapeño and tomato, these baked empanadas are elegant and delicious.

The Damsel Cellars 2015 Stillwater Creek Vineyard Syrah and 2015 Boushey Vineyard Cabernet Franc were both selected to play with the aromas and flavors of the mole sauce. The deep Syrah has aromas and flavors of blueberry, dark cherry, and hints of vanilla with some earthiness and tobacco, and compliments the fruitiness of the dried chili peppers, the sweetness of the spices, and provides a depth of flavor that can hold its own with the mole sauce. The spicy Cabernet Franc has aromas and flavors of red cherry, black raspberry, and dried herbs, complemented by smooth tannins and a well-balanced acidity and acts as a foil to the mole sauce, accenting the heat of the dried chili peppers while its acidity helps clear and refresh the palate for the next bite.

food

Kevin's mole sauce (page 59)
cumin-coriander braised pork (page 60)
empanada dough (page 61)
queso blanco béchamel (page 62)
oregano oil (page 58)
jalapeño oil (page 62)
fresh tomato, cilantro, chilis for garnish

wine

Damsel Cellars
2015 Boushey Vineyard Cabernet Franc
2015 Stillwater Creek Syrah

cooking & plating

1) Make empanadas up to 2 days in advance and freeze.

2) Make oregano and jalapeño oils.

3) Bake empanadas.

4) Make queso blanco béchamel.

5) Remove seeds from tomato and jalapeño, then finely dice.

6) Spread some béchamel sauce on plate and decorate with dots of oregano and jalapeño oils. Place empanadas on plate and garnish with diced fresh tomato and jalapeño, and cilantro, if desired.

---
recipes

empanadas
Kevin's mole sauce
cumin-coriander braised pork
empanada dough
queso blanco béchamel
oregano oil
jalapeño oil

empanadas

1 batch cumin-coriander braised pork
1-1½ c. Kevin's mole sauce
1 batch empanada dough

1) Make braised pork 1 day in advance and refrigerate overnight.

Preheat oven to 375°F.

2) Mix braised pork with 1 c. mole sauce. Filling should hold together and not be soupy. Add a little more mole sauce if needed. Set filling aside.

3) Portion the empanada dough into 1 ounce pieces, forming into balls, and then pressing or rolling out to a 4" diameter circle.

4) Fill with 1-2 Tbl. filling. Fold in half over the filling and crimp the dough to seal. Finish the edge by fluting, folding and braiding (called a "repulgue"), pressing with the tines of a fork, or cutting with a fluted pastry cutter.

5) Bake the empanadas for 20-25 minutes on a sheet pan on the middle rack of the oven until lightly browned, turning pan halfway through to cook and brown evenly.

Makes: 30 large empanadas

The empanadas freeze well, making them easy to handle. If using frozen empanadas, add 5 minutes to the cooking time.

oregano oil

½ c. good quality olive oil
½ c. fresh oregano leaves, loosely packed

1) Combine the oregano and olive oil in a blender. Mix until smooth.

2) Strain the flavored oil through a fine sieve to remove any big bits, if desired, and store in a squeeze bottle for easy use. Keep in the refrigerator for up to 2 weeks.

Makes approximately ½-¾ cup.

Kevin's mole sauce

¼ lb. uncured bacon cut into ¼" pieces
3 ancho chili peppers, seeds and stems removed (reserve seeds)
3 pasilla chili peppers, seeds and stems removed (reserve seeds)
3 mulatto chili peppers, seeds and stems removed (reserve seeds)
3 aji mirasol chili peppers, seeds and stems removed (reserve seeds)
3 guajillo chili peppers, seeds and stems removed (reserve seeds)
¼ c. chili seeds, reserved from seed removal
1 cinnamon stick, broken into small pieces (or 2 tsp. ground)
1 tsp. black peppercorns (or ¼ tsp. ground)
6 allspice berries (or ¼ tsp. ground)
6 whole cloves (or ¼ tsp. ground)
1 tsp. whole coriander seeds
1 tsp. cumin seeds
1 tsp. fennel seeds
3 bay leaves
1 Tbl. olive oil
1 medium sweet onion, chopped (1½ c.)
6 cloves of garlic, coarsely chopped
4-5 plum tomatoes or several round tomatoes, diced (2 c.)
3 fresh tomatillos, husks removed, quartered (about 4 oz.)
1/4 c. raisins
1 tsp. fragrant dried green herbs (oregano, marjoram, or thyme)
1 Tbl. Mexican cane sugar (or brown sugar)
2 tsp. sea salt
4-6 c. water, divided
4-6 oz. Mexican, dark, or bittersweet chocolate (optional)

1) Cook bacon over medium heat until bacon bits are crispy and bacon fat has rendered. Remove the bacon bits and reserve the bacon fat for later.

2) Stem and seed the peppers, reserving ¼ c. of the mixed pepper seeds. Tear the peppers into 1"-2" pieces for easier handling.

3) In a dry skillet over medium heat, roast the dried peppers until they become fragrant, 4-5 minutes. Do this in batches to avoid crowding the pan. Let cool, then place them in a bowl with 2 c. warm water and soak until peppers become soft, 15-20 minutes. Place a small plate on top of the peppers to keep them submerged while soaking. When peppers are softened, puree them together with the soaking water.

4) To bloom the flavors, roast the spices, reserved pepper seeds, and bay leaf in a dry skillet until they become fragrant, 3-4 minutes, being careful not to burn the bay leaf. Let cool.

5) Heat the bacon fat and olive oil in a 4 quart pot over medium high heat. Add onion and sauté until soft, 4-5 minutes. Add garlic when onions are almost done and continue to sauté until the garlic is fragrant, 1 minute.

6) Add tomato, tomatillos, raisins, dried herbs, sugar, and salt. Reduce heat and simmer covered until tomatoes and tomatillos begin to break down, 10-15 minutes. Add water as necessary to keep from burning.

7) Add 2 c. of water, the pureed chili peppers, and the spices to the pot. Stir thoroughly to combine and bring back to a simmer. Simmer covered for 45 minutes.

8) Using an immersion blender, blend until smooth. Or, working in small batches, carefully pour ingredients into a food processor or blender and blend until smooth, then return sauce to pot. Be careful when blending, sauce is hot!

9) Simmer covered for 15 more minutes, stirring occasionally. Add additional water if needed to obtain the desired consistency. Also add the chocolate at this time if you are using it. Let cool, then use, refrigerate, or freeze.

Notes:
- *If you do not like cilantro or coriander (cilantro seeds) leave out the coriander and double the cumin.*
- *For a vegan version use 2-3 Tbl. olive oil instead of the bacon fat and olive oil, and skip step 1.*
- *For a sweeter sauce, use 4 dried cascabel chili peppers instead of the guajillo chili peppers.*
- *Pasilla or guajillo chili peppers can be substitued for aji mirasol peppers.*
- *For additional heat add one or two chipotle chili peppers.*

Makes: approximately 2-3 quarts.

cumin-coriander braised pork

3½-4 lb. pork shoulder roast
1-2 Tbl. olive oil
2 Tbl. ground cumin
2 Tbl. ground coriander
2 tsp. sea salt
¾ -1 c. water

1) Trim the fat from the shoulder roast. Cut roast into 1½" cubes. Add olive oil to pan over medium-high heat and brown meat on several sides. After browning, place meat into a slow cooker or crock pot.

2) Add half of the cumin, half of the coriander, the salt, and enough water to just cover the pork. Stir thoroughly.

3) Cook on high setting for 1 hour, then reduce heat to low setting and cook for 3 more hours. When done, add remaining cumin and coriander and stir to thoroughly combine.

4) If not making empanadas, remove and discard excess fat from the top of the cooked pork shoulder. The braised pork is delicious as a main dish by itself.

5) If making empanada filling, reduce liquid to make a sauce, 30-90 minutes, depending on the amount of liquid. The meat can be removed to speed the reduction. Add the meat back to the pan just before finishing to keep it moist and tender. There should still be a small amount of sauce left when done. Shred, let cool and place in refrigerator overnight.

Makes enough to fill 30 empanadas.

empanada dough

10 oz. all-purpose flour (approx. 2 c.)
5 oz. masa harina or fine corn meal (¾ c.)
¼ oz. sea salt (about ½ tsp.)
6 oz. cold butter cut into small pieces (¾ c.)
9 oz. cold water (approx. ½ cup + 1 Tbl.)

Preheat oven to 425°F.

1) In a large bowl, whisk together flour, masa or fine cornmeal, and salt.

2) Cut in butter with a pastry blender or a fork until the mixture looks like very coarse sand.

3) Make a well in the center of the flour and butter mixture and add the water, mixing to combine. Gently knead until the dough forms a cohesive ball, then continue kneading until dough is smooth, adding small amounts of flour as needed to avoid sticking.

4) Wrap dough with plastic wrap and let rest in the refrigerator for at least 30 minutes or for up to two days before using.

queso blanco béchamel

2 Tbl. all-purpose flour
2 Tbl. butter
1½ c. milk
½ lb monterey jack cheese cut into ¼" pieces
1 pinch salt

1) Place a saucepan over medium high heat, add the butter and flour. Whisk until combined. Continue to whisk until it thickens into a paste and the flour is cooked but not browned, 2-3 minutes.

2) Add the milk and salt, and whisk to combine. Then add the cheese, continuing to whisk slowly as the cheese melts. Once the cheese is melted, continue whisking until the sauce begins to bubble and thicken, 4-5 minutes.

3) Remove from heat and use immediately.

When cooled the sauce will solidify. Simply reheat slowly, adding a little bit more milk if needed and stirring or whisking until it melts and becomes smooth again.

Makes approximately 2 cups.

jalapeño oil

½ c. good quality olive oil
½ c. fresh jalapeño chili peppers, chopped

If less heat is desired, remove chili seeds and white membrane before chopping.

1) Combine the chili peppers and olive oil in a blender. Mix until smooth.

2) Strain the flavored oil through a fine sieve to remove any big bits, if desired, and store in a squeeze bottle for easy use. Keep in the refrigerator for up to 2 weeks.

Makes approximately ½-¾ cup.

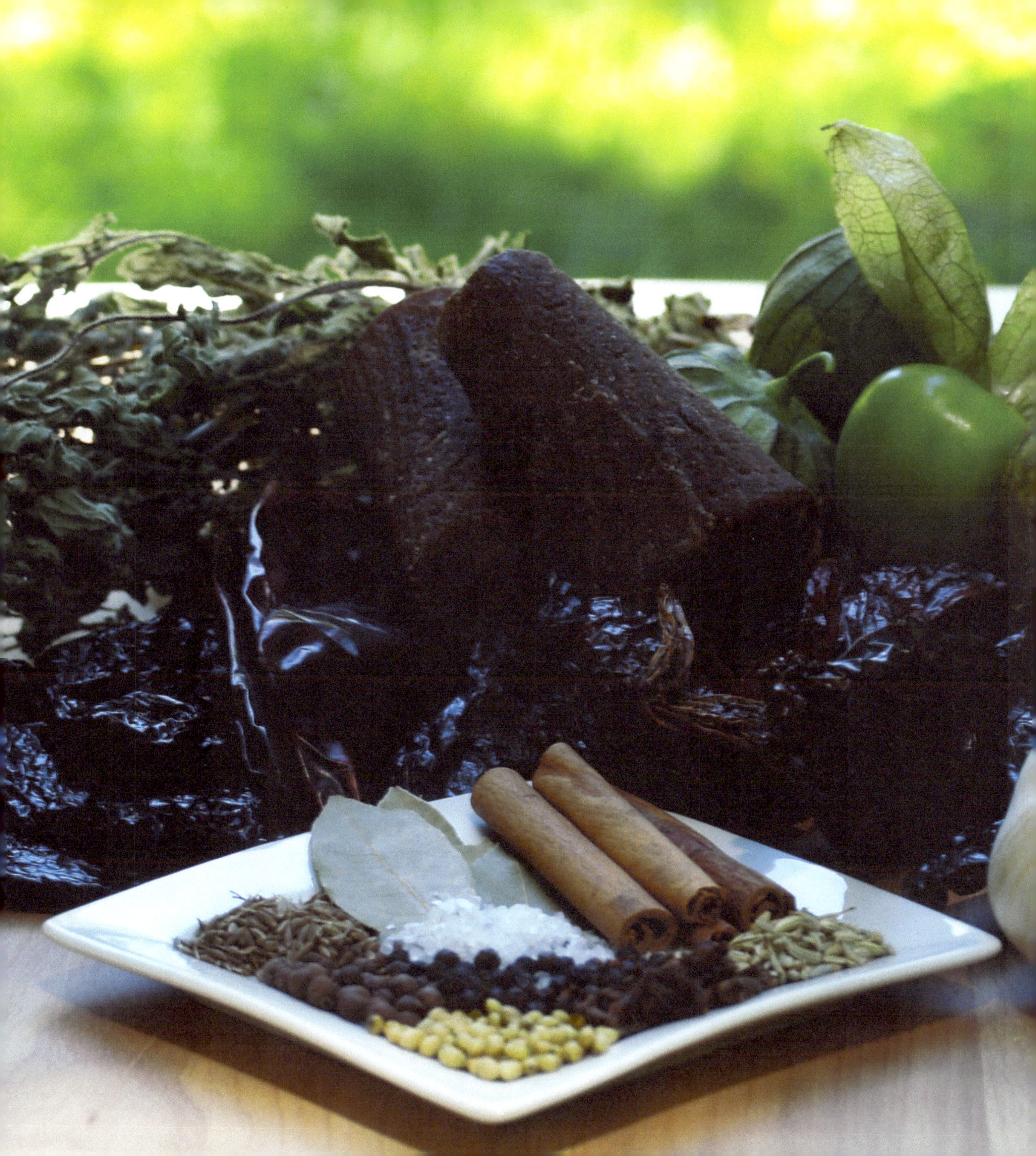

natural

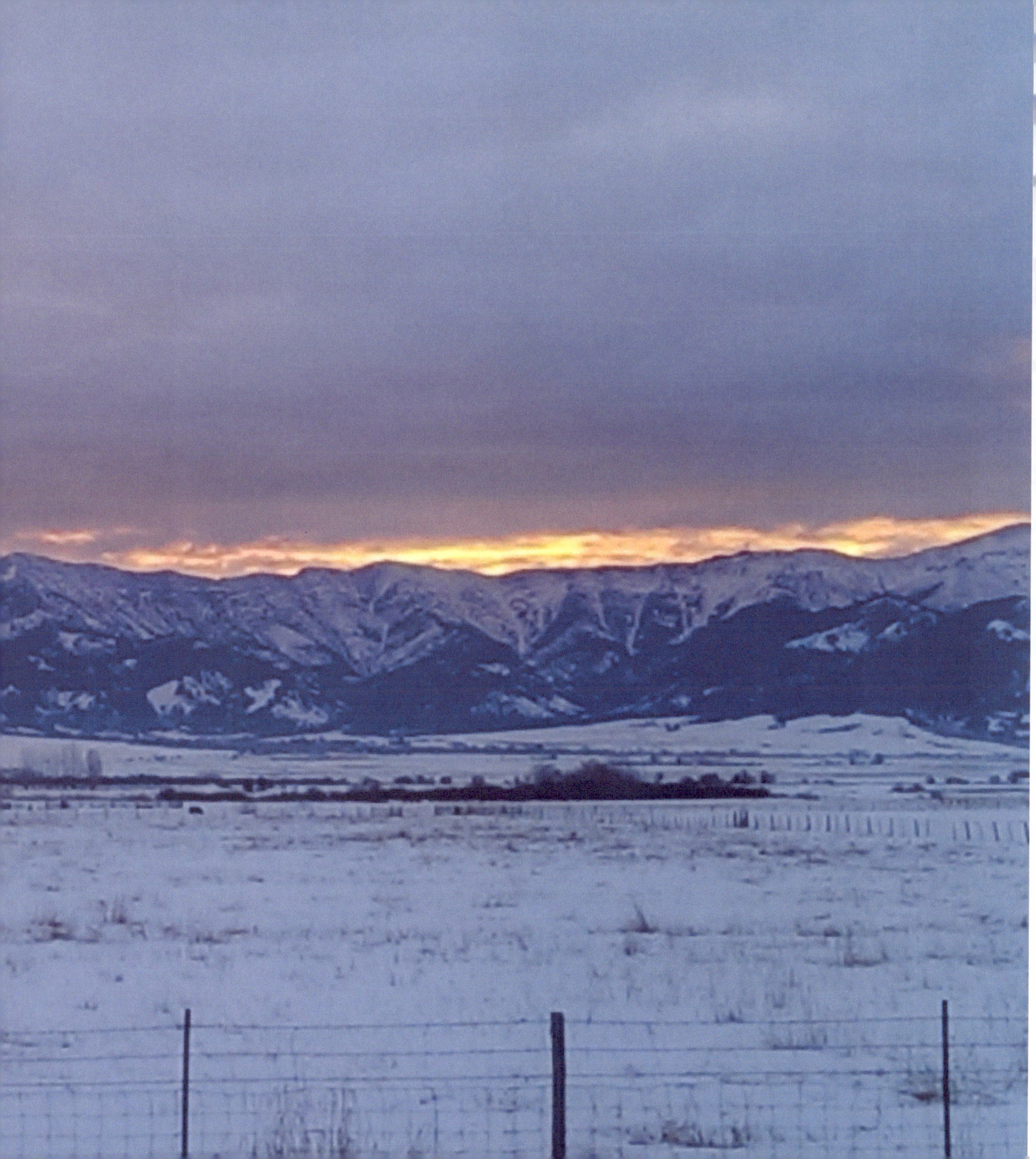

From beautiful wool to delicious grapes, Mother Nature does an amazing job with colors, flavors, and textures. Staying close to the land and developing a connection between family farms and the people that appreciate the care and tradition of a family-produced gorgeous knitting yarn or wonderful wine maintains the relationship to nature many of us miss in our techno-driven lives.

on pins & needles

Tucked between Yellowstone and Glacier National Parks in the gorgeous Gallatin Valley in western Montana is an oasis from hectic modern life. The natural colors of the Shetland x Romney sheep—

ranging from creamy white through fawn and silver to dark charcoal—blend seamlessly into the rolling fields within view of the majestic mountains. Serenity Sheep Farm started when a friend's sheep gave birth to lambs on Shepherdess LaVonne Stucky's birthday and she was able to name them. As LaVonne charmingly says, "I started with two and now there are too many."

The farm-to-fabric model recently got a boost when LaVonne purchased the spinning mill that had been making her yarn and moved it to the farm. The Wool Mill is up and running and makes all the Serenity Sheep Farm yarn, as well as fiber processing and spinning for the public, right there on the farm.

The number of working family farms is rapidly declining. To keep the personal farm experience alive, LaVonne welcomes visitors to the farm. Milk a goat, collect eggs from the chickens, say hi to the turkeys and pigs, and of course pet the sheep. Complete the visit with an overnight stay in the fields in one of the fully refurbished antique shepherd wagons or the cabin.

on the menu

Dusted Valley was founded on the notion that when families work together the American Dream can become a living reality. In 2003, two Wisconsin families with a rich heritage of farming and hospitality — Chad & Janet Johnson and Corey & Cindy Braunel — left their day jobs behind and took a leap of faith to start a new adventure establishing estate vineyards in the Walla Walla Valley and creating Dusted Valley. They haven't looked back since.

Growing up as proud Wisconsin farm kids, Corey is the fourth generation of his family in agriculture and was raised on a ginseng farm in Northern Wisconsin, sisters Janet and Cindy grew up just down the road on their parent's dairy farm, and Chad developed a passion for the wonders of food and wine while working in the hospitality industry. The Wisconsin connection continues today: some of the American oak barrels used to make their wine are from northern Wisconsin where they grew up.

Dusted Valley represents the quest to fulfill their dream of crafting world-class wine in Washington State, living a life that does not revolve around rush hour traffic and corporate deadlines, and where the vineyards and farmlands link us all to our agricultural roots, connecting us to our neighbors every day.

natural

on pins & needles

The gorgeous natural colors of the Serenity Sheep Farm yarn was all the inspiration I needed for the bitterroot pattern. I'd fallen in love with the yarn when I discovered the farm's CSA (community supported agriculture) program many years ago and have been a supporter ever since. The sheep are raised on a family farm and for many years the yarn was spun at a local mill right down the road from the farm. New this year is that the yarn is spun right on the farm – it's hard to get more local than that!

The stitch motif was influenced by thoughts of the ancient Missoula Flood raging through the valley, the more modern thoughts of the sheep walking through the fields, the gorgeous Bitterroot flower that is so prevalent in the area, and the notion of a road trip along scenic byways to visit the place where it all happens.

bitterroot

Sizes
Hat to fit small (medium, large) with finished head circumference: 18¾" (20½", 22¼")
Sweater/vest to fit: 24"-27" (27"-30", 31"-34", 34"-37", 38"-41") [*41"-44", 45"-48", 48"-51", 51"-54"*] bust/chest measurement; worn with neutral to 3" positive ease with finished bust/chest measurement: 27" (30½", 34", 37½", 41") [*44½", 48", 51½", 54¾"*]

Yarn
Sport weight, approx. 300-320 yd/100 g skeins
Hat: 400 yds (200 yds each of c1 and c2)
Sweater: 1200 (1200, 1500, 1500, 1500) [1800, 1800, 1800, 1800] of c1 and 600 yds of c2

Shown in Serenity Sheep Farm yarn, Shetland x Romney wool grown and spun in Montana, ~300 yds / 100 g. Hat shown in charcoal + white, 1 skein each. Sweater shown in moorit + white: 4 (4, 5, 5, 5) [6, 6, 6, 6] skeins of c1 and 2 skeins of c2. Vest shown in silver (c1) + black (c2).

Gauge
28 sts & 28 rounds = 4" (10 cm) in stranded color work, 28 sts & 36 rows/rounds = 4" (10 cm) in stockinette, and 36 sts & 36 rows/rounds = 4" (10 cm) in 2x2 ribbing (easily stretches to same gauge as stockinette) using US 2-5 (2.75-3.75 mm) or size needed to get gauge; different needle sizes may be needed to maintain gauge in different stitches. Gauge measured after blocking. For proper fit, take time to check gauge in color work and stockinette (both flat and in the round), and ribbing.

Notions
stitch markers (some removable), stitch holder/waste yarn, crochet hook or sewing thread/needle + sharp scissors to reinforce steeks, sewing thread to match c1 + needle

Stitches
For stitches and abbreviations, see page 128.

Instructions

Hat

Instructions are given for small (medium, large); when only one number is given it applies to all sizes. Hat is worked in the round.

With c1, cast on 132 (144, 156) sts. Join to knit in the round, being careful not to twist. PM for end of round.

[chart on page 73]

Ribbing Round A: With c1, *k2, p2,* repeat between * around.

Repeat Ribbing Round A until piece measures 2½" or desired length from cast on edge.

Move end of round marker by 1 st as follows: rm, k1-c1, pm for new end of round.

Braid Round 1: With c1, knit. *Join c2.*
Braid Round 2: *K1 with c1, k1 with c2,* repeat between * around.

Bring c1 and c2 to front of work. Increase needle size if needed to keep braid loose but still tidy. Yarn will become twisted on Braid Round 3 and will untwist on Braid Round 4.

[see Braid Rounds 3 & 4 photos on page 74]

Braid Round 3: *Bring c1 under then up and around in front of c2 and p1 with c1; bring c2 under then up and around in front of c1 and p1 with c2,* repeat between * around.
Braid Round 4: *Bring c1 over then down and behind c2 and p1 with c1, bring c2 over then down and behind c1 and p1 with c2,* repeat between * around.
Move c1 and c2 to back of work. Change needle size back to original, if needed.
Braid Round 5: With c1, knit.

ribbing, braid, and stranded color work
same chart is used for sweater and hat

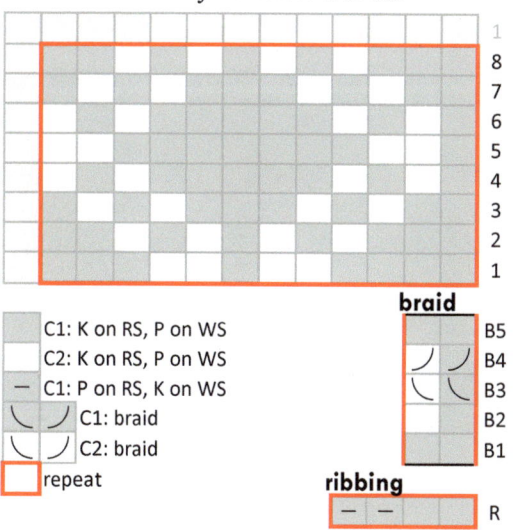

- C1: K on RS, P on WS
- C2: K on RS, P on WS
- — C1: P on RS, K on WS
- C1: braid
- C2: braid
- repeat

braid B1–B5
ribbing R

Begin pattern, changing needle sizes if needed to maintain gauge in color work.

Pattern Round 1: *K4 with c1, k2 with c2, k1 with c1, k2 with c2, k3 with c1,* repeat between * around.
Pattern Round 2: *K3-c1, {k1-c2, k1-c1} 3 times, k1-c2, k2-c1,* repeat between * around.
Pattern Round 3: *K2-c1, k1-c2, k1-c1, k1-c2, k3-c1, k1-c2, k1-c1, k1-c2, k1-c1,* repeat between * around.
Pattern Round 4: *K1-c1, k1-c2, k1-c1, k1-c2, k5-c1, k1-c2, k1-c1, k1-c2,* repeat between * around.
Pattern Round 5: *K1-c1, k2-c2, k7-c1, k2-c2,* repeat between * around.
Pattern Round 6: Repeat Pattern Round 4.
Pattern Round 7: Repeat Pattern Round 3.
Pattern Round 8: Repeat Pattern Round 2.

Repeat Rounds 1-8 two more times or desired length to beginning of crown shaping.
Work Round 1 once to finish pattern. Break c2.

Crown Round 1: With c1, *k12, pm,* repeat between * around.
Crown Round 2 (plain): With c1, knit.
Crown Round 3 (shaping): With c1, *k2tog, k to m, sm,* repeat between * around — 10 (11) sts decreased.

Repeat Crown Rounds 2-3 until 12 sts remain. Break yarn and pass through sts. Fasten off. Weave in ends. Block.

Sweater

*Instructions are given for finished size 27" (30½", 34", 37½", 41") [**44½", 48", 51½", 54¾"**]; when only one number is given it applies to all sizes.*

Sweater body is worked in the round and steeked at sleeve and neck openings. After assembly, neck band stitches are picked up and neck band is worked in the round.

Photos show highlighted text portion of braid in progress.

Braid Round 3: *Bring c1 up and around in front of c2 and p1 with c1, **bring c2 (white) up and around in front of c1 (moorit)** and p1 with c2 (white),* repeat between * around.

Braid Round 4: *Bring c1 down and behind c2 and p1 with c1, **bring c2 (white) down and behind c1 (moorit)** and p1 with c2 (white),* repeat between * around.

Body

With c1, cast on 192 (216, 240, 264, 288) [*312, 336, 360, 384*] sts. Join to knit in the round, being careful not to twist. PM for end of round.

Ribbing Round A: With c1, *k2, p2,* repeat between * around.

Repeat Ribbing Round A until piece measures 3½" or desired length from cast on edge.

Move end of round marker by 1 st as follows: rm, k1-c1, pm for new end of round.

Change to larger needles for Braid, if needed.

Braid Round 1-4: Work Braid Rounds 1-4, same as for Hat (see page 73).
Braid Round 5: With c1, knit 96 (108, 120, 132, 144) [*156, 168, 180, 192*], pm, knit to end of round.

Change back to main working needles, if needed. Begin pattern:

Round 1: *K4 with c1, k2 with c2, k1 with c1, k2 with c2, k3 with c1,* repeat between * around.
Round 2: *K3-c1, {k1-c2, k1-c1} 3 times, k1-c2, k2-c1,* repeat between * around.
Round 3: *K2-c1, k1-c2, k1-c1, k1-c2, k3-c1, k1-c2, k1-c1, k1-c2, k1-c1,* repeat between * around.
Round 4: *K1-c1, k1-c2, k1-c1, k1-c2, k5-c1, k1-c2, k1-c1, k1-c2,* repeat between * around.
Round 5: *K1-c1, k2-c2, k7-c1, k2-c2,* repeat between * around.

Round 6: Repeat Round 4.
Round 7: Repeat Round 3.
Round 8: Repeat Round 2.

Waist shaping

Waist shaping is optional. If no waist shaping is desired, skip to "work even to armhole" section.

Work the k2tog and ssk decreases and the M1L and M1R increases in pattern color.

Continue in established pattern and decrease 4 sts every 4 rounds as follows, beginning on pattern Round 1 (next round):

Decrease Round: K1, k2tog, work in established pattern to 2 sts before m, ssk, sm, k1, k2tog, work in established pattern to 2 sts before m, ssk — 4 sts dec.
Plain Rounds: Work in established pattern for 3 rounds — 0 sts dec.

Repeat Decrease + Plain Rounds four more times — 20 sts decreased, 172 (196, 220, 244, 268) [292, 316, 340, 364] sts total.

Work even in established pattern without decreasing for 1" or desired waist length.

Continue in established pattern and increase 4 sts every 4 rounds as follows:

Increase Round: K1, M1L, work in established pattern to m, M1R, sm, k1, M1L, work in established pattern to m, M1R — 4 sts inc.
Plain Rounds: Work in established pattern for 3 rounds — 0 sts inc.

*Repeat Increase + Plain Rounds four more times — 20 sts increased, 192 (216, 240, 264, 288) [**312, 336, 360, 384**] sts total.*

Work even to armhole

If no waist shaping is desired, resume here.

*Continue in established pattern and work even until piece measures 14½" (15", 15¼", 15½", 15¾") [**16", 16¼", 16½", 16¾"**] or desired length to armhole.*

For steek stitches, cast on using backward loop.

Separate front back, start armhole and neck shaping, and add steek stitches:
Continuing in established pattern, work 48 (54, 60, 66, 72) [**78, 84, 90, 96**] sts across left front to center stitch, k1 with c1 for center stitch, pm, co-5 sts onto right needle in c1-c2-c1-c2-c1 for neck opening steek, pm, M1L with c1, work 42 (48, 54, 60, 63) [**69, 75, 81, 85**] sts across right front, pm, co-5 sts with c2 for armhole steek onto right needle, pm, bind off 11 (11, 11, 11, 17) [**17, 17, 17, 23**] sts for underarm with c1, work 85 (97, 109, 121, 127) [**139, 151, 163, 169**] sts in established pattern across back, pm, co-5 sts with c2 for armhole steek onto right needle, pm, bind off 11 (11, 11, 11, 17) [**17, 17, 17, 23**] sts for underarm with c1, pm for end of round — 43 (49, 55, 61, 64) [**70, 76, 82, 85**] sts on each front and 85 (97, 109, 121, 127) [**139, 151, 163, 169**] sts on back; stitch counts do not include steek sts.

Next Round: *Work in established pattern to m, sm, k1-c1, k1-c2, k1-c1, k1-c2, k1-c1 for steek sts, sm,* repeat between * around.

Continue in established pattern and AT THE SAME TIME begin armhole and neck shaping decreasing 6 sts every other round as follows, working k2tog and ssk in pattern color:

Decrease Round: *K1-c1, k2tog, work in established pattern to 3 sts before m, ssk, k1-c1, sm, k1-c1, k1-c2, k1-c1, k1-c2, k1-c1 for steek sts, sm,* repeat between * around — 6 sts dec (2 at neck and 2 at each underarm).
Plain Round: *Work in established pattern to m, sm, k1-c1, k1-c2, k1-c1, k1-c2, k1-c1 for steek sts, sm,* repeat between * around — 0 sts dec.

*Repeat Decrease + Plain Round five more times — 36 sts decreased; 30 (36, 42, 48, 54) [**55, 61, 68, 73**] sts on each front and 71 (83, 95, 107, 119) [**121, 133, 125, 157**] sts on back.*

Continue in established pattern and AT THE SAME TIME stop armhole shaping and continue neck shaping decreasing 2 sts every other round at neck edge as follows, working k2tog and ssk in pattern color:

Decrease Round: Work in established pattern to 3 sts before m, ssk, k1-c1, sm, k1-c1, k1-c2, k1-c1, k1-c2, k1-c1 for steek sts, sm, k1-c1, k2tog, work in established pattern to m, sm, k1-c1, k1-c2, k1-c1, k1-c2, k1-c1 for steek sts, sm, work in established pattern across back to m, sm, k1-c1, k1-c2, k1-c1, k1-c2, k1-c1 for steek sts, sm — 2 sts dec at neck.
Plain Round: *Work in established pattern to m, sm, k1-c1, k1-c2, k1-c1, k1-c2, k1-c1 for steek sts, sm,* repeat between * to end — 0 sts dec.

Repeat Decrease + Plain Round until piece measures 6" (6½", 7", 7½", 8") [8½", 9", 9½", 10"] or ¾" less than desired length from beginning of armhole, ending with plain round. There will be 21 (23, 24, 26, 28) [30, 31, 33, 35] sts remaining on each front.

Continue in established pattern of v-neck decreases and AT THE SAME TIME begin back neck shaping:

Neck Round 1 (back neck opening): Work in established pattern to 3 sts before m, ssk, k1-c1, sm, k1-c1, k1-c2, k1-c1, k1-c2, k1-c1 for steek sts, sm, k1-c1, k2tog, work in established pattern to m, sm, work 21 (23, 24, 26, 28) [30, 31, 33, 35] sts across right back, pm, co-5 sts with c2 for back neck steek onto right needle, pm, bind off 41 (45, 47, 51, 55) [59, 61, 65, 69] sts for back neck with c1, work 21 (23, 24, 26, 28) [30, 31, 33, 35] sts in established pattern across left back to end.

Neck Round 2 (plain): *Work in established pattern to m, sm, k1-c1, k1-c2, k1-c1, k1-c2, k1-c1 for steek sts, sm,* repeat between * to end.

Neck Round 3 (shaping): *Work in established pattern to 3 sts before m, ssk, k1-c1, sm, k1-c1, k1-c2, k1-c1, k1-c2, k1-c1 for steek sts, sm, k1-c1, k2tog, work in established pattern to m, sm, k1-c1, k1-c2, k1-c1 for steek sts, sm,* repeat between * once more across back.

Neck Round 4 (plain): *Work in established pattern to m, sm, k1-c1, k1-c2, k1-c1, k1-c2, k1-c1 for steek sts, sm,* repeat between * to end.

Reinforce steeks (photo 1 + 2), cut steeks (photo 3).

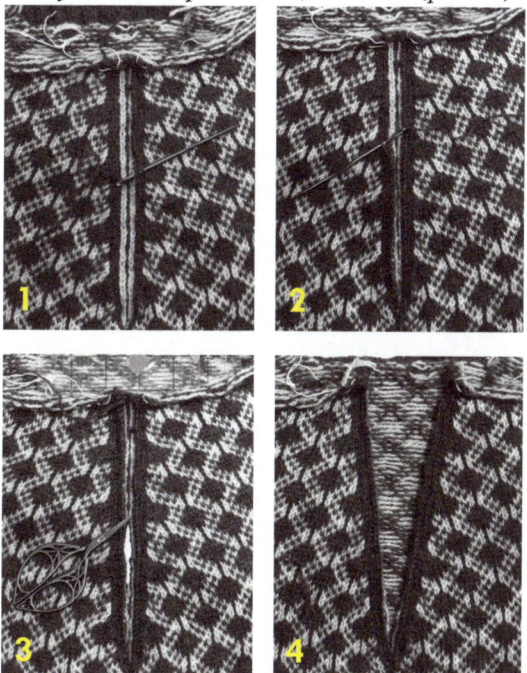

Neck Round 5 (shaping and steek bind off):
Work in established pattern to 3 sts before m, ssk, k1-c1, rm, bo-5 steek sts in color pattern, rm, k1-c1, k2tog, work in established pattern to m, rm, bo-5 steek sts, rm, repeat between * once more across back.

Piece measures 6¾" (7¼", 7¾", 8¼", 8¾") [9¼", 9¾", 10¼", 10¾"] from beginning of armhole.

Place all sts on holder/waste yarn.
Weave in ends. Block body.

Reinforce and cut steeks (see photos on page 77).

Using c1, graft or 3-needle bind off shoulder seams.

Using c2, duplicate stitch pattern stitches as needed over shoulder seam stitches, if desired.

Sleeves

Cuff is worked in ribbing with a contrasting color cast on and then remainder of sleeve is worked in stockinette in the round to armhole, then worked flat. Sleeves are identical. Make 2.

For vest, skip to Sleeve band for vest section (page 79).

With c2, cast on cast on 56 (56, 60, 64, 68) [72, 76, 80, 80] sts. Join to knit in the round, being careful not to twist. PM for end of round.

Setup Round: With c2, *k2, p2,* repeat between * around.
Break c2. Join c1.
Remainder of sleeve is worked in c1.

Cuff Round (ribbing): With c1, *k2, p2,* repeat between * around.

Repeat Cuff Round until piece measures 3½" or desired length.

Sleeve setup (shift end of round): Remove marker, k1, pm for new end of round. With c1, knit 4 rounds.

Continue to work sleeves in stockinette (knit all sts), and AT THE SAME TIME increase 2 sts every 10 (10, 10, 8, 8) [8, 8, 8, 6] rows as follows:

Sleeve Increase Round: K2, M1L, knit to 2 sts before marker, M1R, k2 — 2 sts inc.
Sleeve Plain Rounds: Work 9 (9, 9, 7, 7) [7, 7, 7, 5] rows in stockinette without increasing.

Repeat sleeve increase + plain rounds until there are 78 (78, 84, 92, 98) [102, 108, 112, 120] sts.

Work even in stockinette without increasing until sleeve measures 17" (17", 18", 18", 18") [19", 19", 19", 19"] from cast on or is 2 rounds less than desired length to under arm.

Underarm bind off Round 1: Bind off 6 (6, 6, 6, 9) [9, 9, 9, 12] sts, knit to end of round. Turn work so that wrong side is facing.

Remainder of sleeve is worked flat.

Underarm bind off Row 2 (WS): Bind off 6 (6, 6, 6, 9) [9, 9, 9, 12] sts, knit to end of row — 66 (66, 72, 80, 80) [84, 90, 94, 96] sts.

Continue to work sleeves in stockinette and AT THE SAME TIME decrease 2 sts every 3 rows as follows:

Sleeve Cap Row 1 (RS, dec): K2, ssk, knit to 4 sts before end, k2tog, k2 — 2 sts dec.
Sleeve Cap Rows 2-3: Work in stockinette.
Sleeve Cap Row 4 (WS, dec): P2, p2tog, purl to 4 sts before end, ssp, p2 — 2 sts dec.
Sleeve Cap Rows 5-6: Work in stockinette.

Repeat Sleeve Cap Rows 1-6 two more times — 12 sts dec, 54 (54, 60, 68, 68) [72, 78, 82, 84] sts.

Work sleeve cap even in stockinette without decreasing until sleeve cap measures 4" (4", 4¾", 5½", 6") [6", 6", 6¾", 6¾"] from underarm bind off rows or ½" less than desired length.

Bind off 12 sts at beginning of next 4 rows. Bind off remaining sts. Block sleeves. Sew sleeve seams and set in sleeves.

Sleeve band for vest

With right side facing, beginning at center bottom of armhole opening and using c1 for matching band or c2 for contrast band, pick up and knit about 9 sts for every 10 rows or stitches around armhole — 96 (100, 108, 116, 124) [132, 140, 144, 156] sts (number of stitches should be a multiple of 4). PM for end of round and join to knit in the round.

Sleeve Band Round (ribbing): Starting with bottom center st, *k2, p2,* repeat between * around.

Repeat Sleeve Band Round until band measures ¾" or desired length.

Bind off in pattern. Repeat for other sleeve band.

Neck band

Neck Band Round 1: *Join c1 and c2.* With right side facing and starting at center back, *pick up and knit 1 in c1, pu&k1 in c2,* repeat between * picking up 1 st for every row and stitch along left back neck then left front neck line to center front, pm, continue in next color and pu&k 1 st in center of "v" for center front, pm, continue in next color and maintain alternating color sequence and pu&k 1 st for every row and stitch along right front neck then back neck all the way to center back, pm for end of round — 126 (134, 142, 152, 160) [*170, 178, 186, 196*] sts (total number of sts should be even).

Change to larger needles for Braid, if needed. For a simple neckband braid:

Neck Band Rounds 2-3 (simple braid): Work Braid Rounds 3-4 same as for Hat.

For mirrored braid as shown in sweater and vest in photos, work as follows:

Neck Band Round 2 (mirrored): Work Braid Round 3 same as for Hat to center front stitch then switch to work Braid Round 4 same as for Hat to center back.

Neck Band Round 3 (mirrored): Work Braid Round 4 same as for Hat to center front stitch then switch to work Braid Round 3 same as for Hat to center back.

Break c2, remainder of neck band is worked with c1. Change back to working needles, if needed.

Neck Band Round 4: With c1, knit.

For a neat and stable neck band, the next round will decrease approximately 1 st for every 9 existing sts. Count sts so that a k3 worked as <k1—m—k1 center st—m—k1> is centered in the front of v-neck.

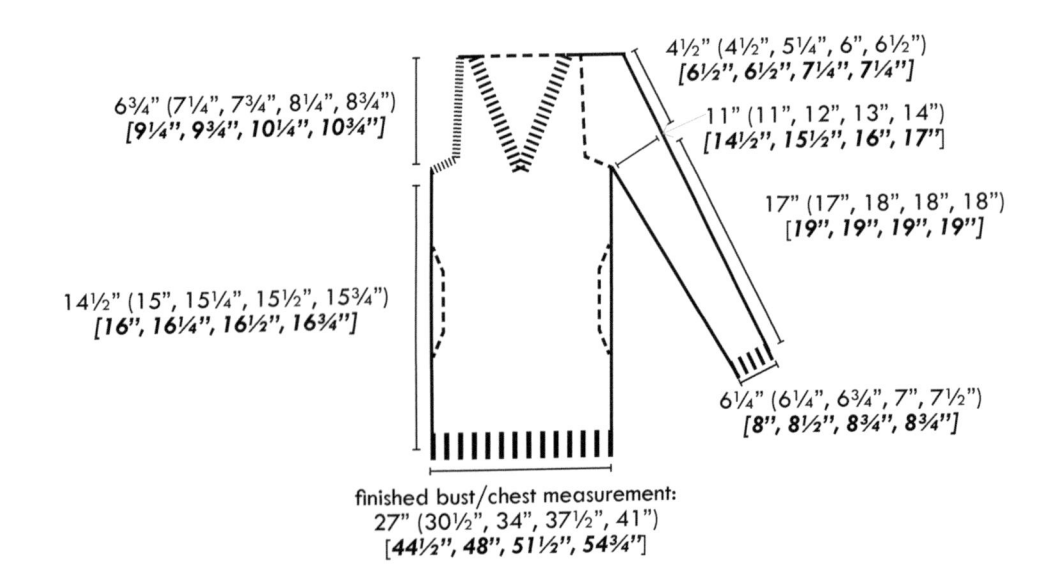

6¾" (7¼", 7¾", 8¼", 8¾") [*9¼", 9¾", 10¼", 10¾"*]

4½" (4½", 5¼", 6", 6½") [*6½", 6½", 7¼", 7¼"*]

11" (11", 12", 13", 14") [*14½", 15½", 16", 17"*]

17" (17", 18", 18", 18") [*19", 19", 19", 19"*]

14½" (15", 15¼", 15½", 15¾") [*16", 16¼", 16½", 16¾"*]

6¼" (6¼", 6¾", 7", 7½") [*8", 8½", 8¾", 8¾"*]

finished bust/chest measurement:
27" (30½", 34", 37½", 41") [*44½", 48", 51½", 54¾"*]

Neck Band Round 5 (decrease): Working so that a p2 of the ribbing will end 1 st before first center stitch marker, *k2, p2tog, p1, k2, p2,* repeat between * to 1 st before marker, k1, sm, k1 for center st, sm, k1, p2, *k2, p2tog, p1, k2, p2,* repeat between * to end of round. If needed, fudge the decreases a bit by replacing a p2tog with a p1 or adding a p2tog so that the round will end with a p2 or <p2tog, p1> and have a continuous flow to the next round — about 1 st decreased every 9 sts, 112 (120, 128, 140, 148) [*152, 160, 168 176*] sts (total number of stitches should be a multiple of 4).

Neck Band Round 6 : Work in established *k2, p2,* ribbing pattern to 2 sts before first center front marker, ssk, sm, k1, sm, k2tog, then continue in established ribbing pattern to end of round — 2 sts dec.

Neck Band Round 7: Work in established *k2, p2,* ribbing pattern to 1 st before first center front marker, k1, sm, k1, sm, k1, then continue in established ribbing pattern to end of round.

Repeat Neck Band Rounds 6-7 until band measures 1" from beginning of braid, or desired length, ending on Neck Band Round 6.

Bind off in pattern. Weave in ends. Block neck band.

Facings

With wrong side facing, use sewing thread and needle to tack steek facings to wrong side of work, if desired.

pura

on the menu

This food and wine pairing began with a hot lemongrass salsa verde. Thinly sliced braised flank steak on a multi-layer stacked corn tortilla tostada with Monterey jack cheese provides the perfect delivery mechanism for the salsa: melding the flavors of caramelized slow cooked steak, sweet fragrant corn, and slightly tangy, creamy melted cheese with the hot, citrusy, lemongrass of the salsa. Sour cream cole slaw rounds out the dish, adding a cooling crunch to help with the heat from the salsa.

The Dusted Valley 2016 Olsen Vineyard Chardonnay is crisp, floral, and bright with notes of citrus, particularly lemon and lime zest, with a slightly creamy texture and pairs perfectly with the aromas and flavors of the salsa and corn tortillas, as well as providing a palate cleansing counterpoint to the flank steak and slaw.

The 2015 Malbec is earthy with structured tannins and aromas and flavors of red and black fruit, blackberries, bing cherry, and dried herbs, reinforcing the earthy and caramel flavors of the braised flank steak, with red fruit as counterpoint, while maintaining its integrity with the salsa and slaw.

food

scallywag sauce (page 85)
braised flank steak (page 86)
corn tortillas
queso fresco
Monterey jack cheese
sour cream cole slaw (page 87)
whole jalapeño peppers
fresh cilantro and ginger

wine

Dusted Valley
2014 Columbia Valley Malbec
2016 Olsen Vineyard Chardonnay

cooking & plating

1) Make scallywag sauce up to 3 days in advance.

2) Make braised flank steak up to 1 day in advance.

3) Preheat oven to 400°F. Layer corn tortilla, thinly sliced flank steak, scallywag sauce, and Monterey jack cheese. Repeat 2 more times for a stack of 3 layers. Bake for 25-30 minutes until cheese is melted and food is hot.

4) While stacks are baking, slice one jalapeño in half lengthwise and pan roast it on both sides to add some color for decoration. Thinly slice another jalapeño for garnish; remove seeds to reduce heat if desired. Chop cilantro. Slice ginger.

5) Cut each stack into 4 pieces, arrange on plates, garnish with cilantro, sliced chilis, and ginger. Add a spoonful of cole slaw.

---
recipes
---

scallywag sauce
braised flank steak
sour cream cole slaw

scallywag sauce

5-6 serrano chili peppers, stems removed
6-10 tomatillos, fresh (husks removed) or
   24-28 oz. can, drained and rinsed
3-4 cloves of garlic, skins on
2"-3" ginger root, peeled, coarsely chopped
2-3 stalks lemongrass, cores only, sliced thinly
   then coarsely minced
1½ c. water
1 lime, juiced and zest minced
¼ c. sugar
1½ tsp. sea salt
½ c. apple cider vinegar

1)   Place ginger root, lemongrass, and water in a 4-quart pot. Bring to a boil, then reduce heat to a simmer. Cover and simmer until the lemongrass is soft, 1-1½ hours.

2)   In a separate pan, dry roast the garlic, serrano chili peppers, and fresh tomatillos for 5-10 minutes until slightly blackened and fragrant. *[If using canned tomatillos, do not pan roast them.]* Remove pan from heat and set aside to cool.

3)   When cooled, peel garlic. Coarsely chop the serrano chili peppers and garlic. Combine tomatillos, serranos, and garlic in a bowl.

85

4)   Once the lemongrass is softened, add serrano-garlic-tomatillo mixture, lime juice, lime zest, sugar, and salt to the lemongrass-ginger pot. Bring back to a boil, reduce heat and simmer covered for approximately 30 minutes to soften the chili peppers, garlic, and tomatillos.

5)   Add vinegar to the pot. Using an immersion blender, blend until smooth. Or, working in small batches, carefully pour ingredients into a food processor or blender and blend until smooth, then return sauce to pot. Be careful when blending, sauce is hot! Add more water, if needed, for desired consistency.

6)   Simmer covered for 15 more minutes, stirring occasionally. Let cool, then use, refrigerate, or freeze.

Makes approximately 1-1½ quarts.

braised flank steak

2-2½ lbs. flank steak
2 Tbl. olive oil
1 Tbl. sea salt
2 tsp. freshly ground black pepper
¾ -1 c. water
1" ginger, minced (optional)

Preheat oven to 275°F.

1)   Cut flank steak with the grain into 3"-4" wide pieces and to fit a 9" x 13" baking dish or a casserole, keeping the pieces separated. Freeze the flank steak pieces for 3-4 hours or overnight.

2)   Working with a few pieces at a time and keeping the remainder frozen until needed, season the top and bottom of the frozen flank steak pieces with salt and pepper.

3)   Heat a large sauté pan over medium high to high heat and add olive oil. When the oil shimmers add seasoned, frozen flank steak pieces in batches to avoid crowding the pan and sear until brown on both sides, 4-5 minutes per side. Don't play with them, let the crust form! Once the top and bottom are seared, remove to baking dish or casserole. Add more oil if necessary for later batches.

4)   Add enough water to reach halfway up the side of the flank steak in the baking dish or casserole. Add the minced ginger to the water. Tightly seal with foil.

5)   Place flank steak on middle rack of oven and let cook for 1½-2 hours. It should be very tender when done.

6)   If using immediately, let rest for 5-10 minutes and then thinly slice across the grain or shred for the tostadas or tacos. Otherwise, refrigerate whole pieces for slicing or shred while hot and refrigerate.

Makes enough for 10-12 single layer tostadas or tacos, or 3-4 stacked tostadas.

sour cream cole slaw

2 lbs. green cabbage thinly sliced (6 c.)
¾ lb. purple cabbage thinly sliced (2 c.)
3 medium carrots (about 1½-2 c.)
2 stalks celery, minced (1 c.)
1 c. sour cream
¼ c. apple cider vinegar
¼ c. sugar
1 Tbl. sea salt
½ tsp. finely ground black pepper

1) Cut cabbage into quarters and remove the core from each quarter. Cut each quarter into very thin slices, about ⅛" thick, and cross cut to get pieces that are 1-1½" long. Place the sliced cabbage into a large mixing bowl.

2) Shred or julienne the carrots into 1" long pieces that are the same width as the cabbage and add to bowl.

3) Finely mince the celery and add it to the bowl with the cabbage and carrot.

4) In a separate bowl, mix together sour cream, apple cider vinegar, sugar, salt, and pepper and stir to thoroughly combine all of the ingredients. Stir into cabbage mix.

5) Let rest in the refrigerator for at least 1 hour, preferably overnight.

6) Before serving, stir well and test for seasoning. Add salt or pepper if desired.

Makes 3-4 quarts.

speke

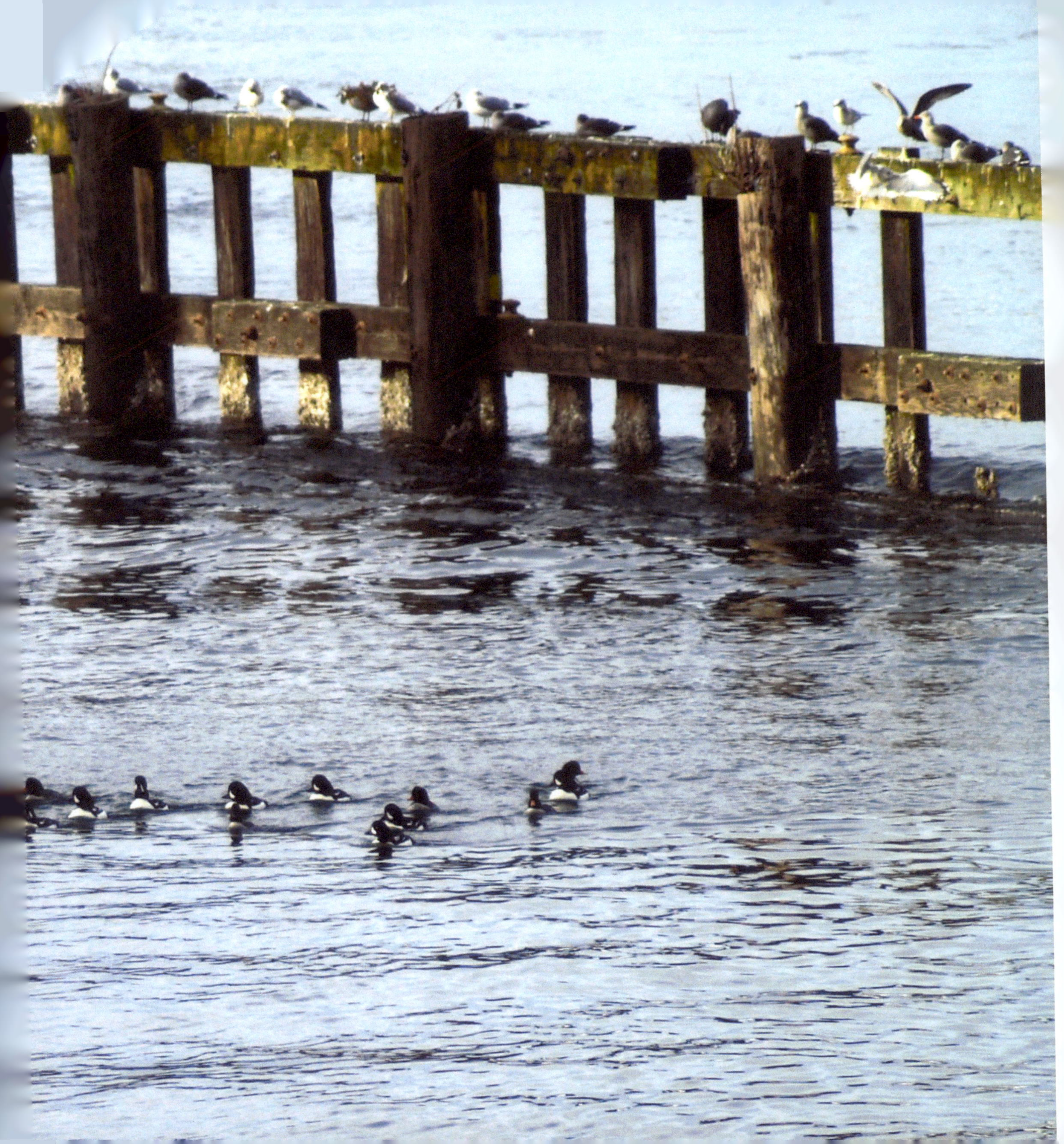

Collaboration builds businesses and when family and friends come together and collaborate, extraordinary businesses can be created.

on pins & needles

One of the first things I notice when looking at a wall of NanoStitch Lab yarns is the incredible range of colors and how beautifully they all work together.

Mad scientists Angela Wallace and Heather Gibbs will be the first to tell you that they aren't "real" scientists, but when they suit up in safety masks, gloves, and aprons to get their speckle on, they sure feel like it! These creative friends joined forces to bring us stunning hand-painted speckled yarns inspired by science and celebrating women in STEM (science, technology, engineering, and math). Their yarn can be found in their online shop and at several local retailers and fiber fests. Their *Science is Real* monthly club is a hot ticket, and they're currently in the process of hosting their first *Yarn Revolution* local fiber festival. This is a fantastic young company and one to watch.

on the menu

At Sparkman Cellars, the warm Southern-style greeting is as welcome as the wine. Sparkman's long and successful history in the hospitality business is clearly visible in the attentiveness of the knowledgeable and friendly staff and the exceptional quality and variety of the wines.

Family is the driving force in Chris and Kelly Sparkman's life and starting the winery in 2004 allowed them to focus on their family. The love of family threads its way through all aspects of Sparkman Cellars, including the naming of the wines, with some bearing family names and others like Outlaw, Holler, and Kindred evoking their Southern heritage and family stories. The first Stella Mae (wine), named for the first daughter, was Syrah-based but when Ruby Leigh came along the wines became "sisters" and changed to Left Bank and Right Bank Bordeaux-style blends. The wine family gets two new names this year, adding Baba and Gaga as a tribute to the grandmothers.

We have many favorite stories involving Sparkman wines and a particular favorite is about the Hallelujah port. At the conclusion of one of our rather festive dinner parties, we brought out various libations with the dessert course. The port was so popular that we finished the bottle and it only took a little prompting before we all threw our hands in the air and shouted "Hallelujah!"

The amazing wine and great people keep us coming back to Sparkman Cellars where every day their motto rings true: "Family. Good Livin'. Damn Fine Wine."

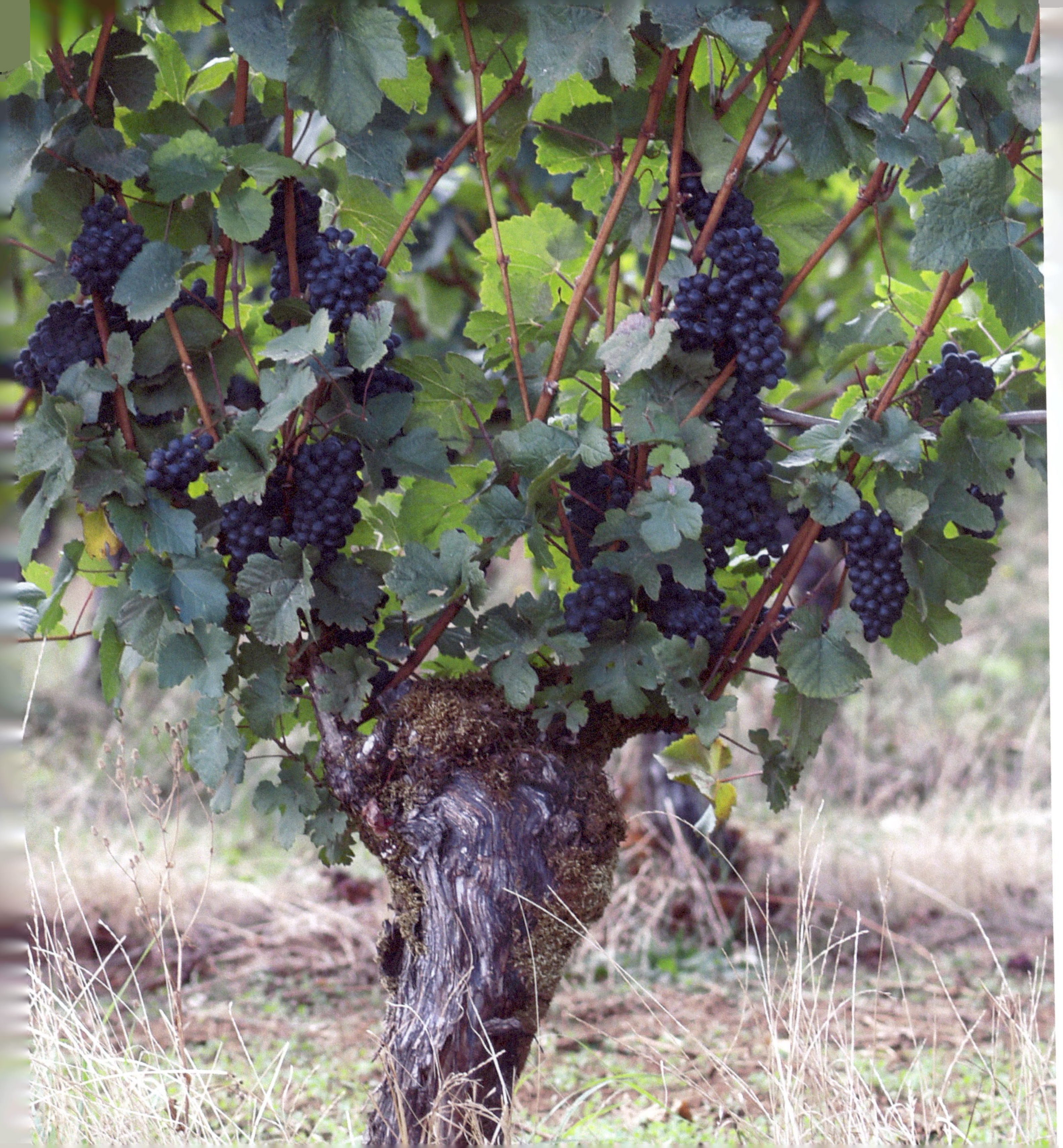

speckle

on pins & needles

My design process begins with inspiration: sometimes it starts with a feeling or an object or a view, sometimes it starts with a color or texture or yarn, and sometimes—as in the case of this pattern—it starts with a stitch.

I was playing around with this swirly stitch and swatching in fingering and worsted weights when I realized that it was pretty but needed something extra...it needed to be BIG!

The harmonious colors and gorgeous speckles of Nano Stitch Lab yarns immediately sprang to mind and I was happy to learn they had a base that would be perfect: Big Bang!

Big yarn, big color, and a big shape all give the cassiopeia cowl a big impact.

cassiopeia

Sizes
Small cowl: 25" circumference x 11½" deep (60 x 30 cm)
Large cowl: 40" circ x 11½" d (105 x 20 cm)
Loop: 50" circ x 8½" d (125 x 25 cm)

Yarn
Bulky weight, 300 (450, 450) yds total: 150 (225, 225) yds in each of 2 colors

Shown in NanoStitch Lab Big Bang Super Bulky (76 yds / 100 g). Large cowl: Gravity + Dark Matter, 3 skeins each; Small cowl: Refraction + Oxygen; 2 skeins each.

Gauge
11½ sts & 16 rounds = 4" (10 cm) in pattern after blocking using US 11-17 (8-11 mm) or size needed to get gauge.

Gauge is not critical for this project; a different gauge will yield a different size and have different yarn requirements.

Notions
stitch marker

Stitches
For standard stitches, see page 128.

Instructions

Instructions are given for small cowl (large cowl, loop); when only one number is given it applies to all sizes.

Cowls and loop are worked in the round. Carry unused color loosely up inside of work.

Special Stitches

[See photos on page 98.]

✳ **supernova** — slip 5 sts to right needle as if to purl, dropping YOs; slip same 5 sts back to left needle; keeping original 5 sts on left needle until stitch is complete {knit 5 together - yo - knit the same 5 sts tog - yo - knit the same 5 sts tog} all into the same 5 sts — stitch count remains the same

↓ **knit with loose strands** — with left needle tip at back of work, lift the strands carried by slipped stitches of 2 previous rows onto left needle, knit the loose strands from previous 2 rounds together with the next stitch — stitch count remains the same

Cast on

With c1 using knitted cast on method, cast on 72 (114, 144) sts.

Join to knit in the round, being careful not to twist. PM for end of round.

Setup Round: With c1, purl. *Join c2.*

Round 1: With c2, *{yo, k1} 5 times, sl-1 wyib,* repeat between * around.
Round 2: With c2, *work supernova, sl-1 wyib,* repeat between * around.
Round 3: With c1, *k5, knit next st together with the 2 loose strands on back of work,* repeat between * around.
Round 4: With c1, purl.
RM, sl-3, replace marker for new beginning of round.

Repeat Rounds 1-4: 1 (1, 0) more time(s) — 9 (9, 5) rounds in total.

supernova

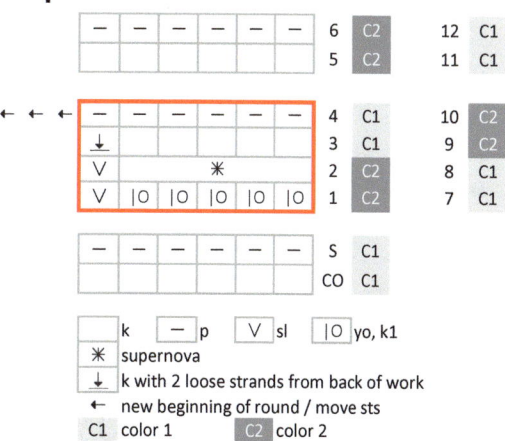

—	—	—	—	—	—	6	C2
						5	C2
—	—	—	—	—	—	4	C1
↓						3	C1
V			✳			2	C2
V	O	O	O	O	O	1	C2

						12	C1
						11	C1
						10	C2
						9	C2
						8	C1
						7	C1

| — | — | — | — | — | — | S | C1 |
| | | | | | | CO | C1 |

| □ k | — p | V sl | O yo, k1 |
| ✳ supernova |
| ↓ k with 2 loose strands from back of work |
| ← new beginning of round / move sts |
| C1 color 1 | C2 color 2 |

97

Round 5: With c2, knit.
Round 6: With c2, purl.

Round 7: With c1, repeat Round 1.
Round 8: With c1, repeat Round 2.
Round 9: With c2, repeat Round 3.
Round 10: With c2, repeat Round 4.
RM, sl-3, replace marker for new beginning of round.

Repeat Rounds 7-10: 6 (6, 4) more times, continuing to move beginning of round 3 sts left at end of Round 10 — 39 (39, 27) total rounds worked from beginning.

Round 11: With c1, knit.
Round 12: With c1, purl.

Work Rounds 1-4: 1 (1, 0) time(s), then Rounds 1-3 one time — 48 (48, 32) rounds total. Do not move marker on last repeat. Break c2.

Bind off and finishing

With c1, purl bind off as follows: *p2tog, slip st back to left needle,* repeat between * around. Weave in ends. Block.

Photos at far left:

✳ supernova stitch — slip, dropping YOs, and slip 5 sts back to right needle (1); k5tog keeping sts on left needle (2); full stitch complete and ready to naturally move off left needle and onto right needle (3)

Photos at near left:

↓ knit with loose strands — pick up 2 strands (1 + 2 show back of work, 3 shows front of work); knit next stitch together with strands (4)

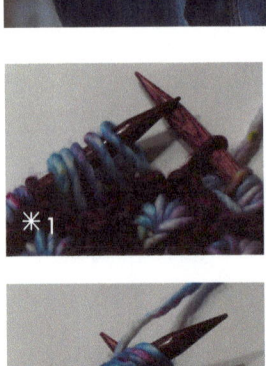

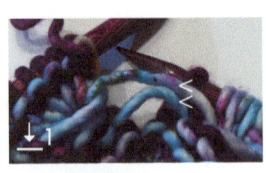

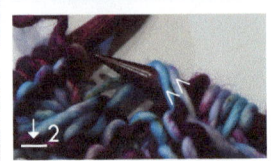

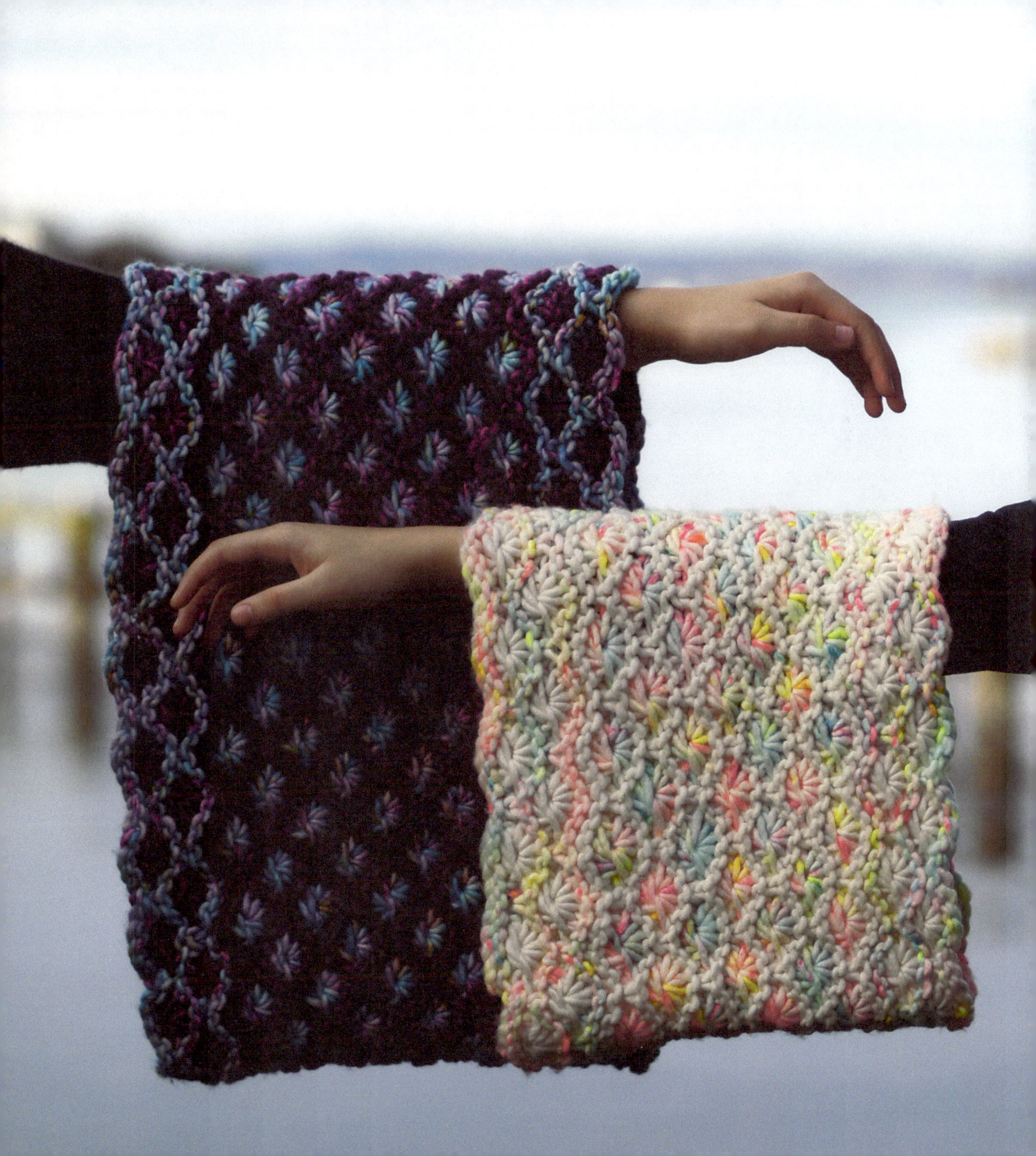

sparkle

on the menu

These recipes began with the idea of infusing the flavors and aromas of lemongrass into different cuts of meat.

The first dish is a classic meat and potatoes dish with a lemongrass twist. Sparkman Cellars "sisters" wines—the 2013 Ruby Leigh Merlot blend and 2013 Stella Mae Cabernet Sauvignon blend—both pair well with the caramel flavors and sweetness of the pork, while the lemongrass and gremolata provide contrasting flavors and a strong herbal component. Don't let anyone tell you asparagus doesn't go with red wine; it just needs a little bit of love (also known as butter and garlic!). The Ruby Leigh is floral, with aromas and flavors of dark cherry and blueberry, smooth tannins, and a savory earthiness that makes this wine an excellent choice with seared meats. The Stella Mae has aromas and flavors of cherry and black raspberry, with hints of cedar and dried herbs, well-structured, elegant tannins, and is velvety and delicious.

The second dish is a play on three distinct lemon flavors: lemongrass, lemon juice, and lemon zest. The crisp and refreshing 2016 Lumière Chardonnay is wild yeast fermented, producing a variety of complex fruit forward flavors, including lemon zest, apple, and pear, with a creamy texture and nice acidity, adding another lemon flavor to the pasta al limone experience.

food

lemongrass smoked+infused pork tenderloin
(page 103)
pasta al limone (page 104)
gremolata (page 104)

wine

Sparkman Cellars
2013 Stella Mae
2013 Ruby Leigh
2016 Lumière Chardonnay

cooking & plating

1) Make pork tenderloin up to 1 day in advance and refrigerate overnight.

For pasta and white wine pairing:
    a. Make pasta al limone and crispy shredded pork.

    b. Plate pasta, top with crispy shredded pork, and garnish with smoked salt and chopped basil.

For medallions and red wine pairing:
    a. Make mashed potatoes, pork medallions, and asparagus.

    b. Place mashed potatoes on plate, arrange medallions and asparagus, and garnish with gremolata.

recipes

lemongrass infused pork tenderloin
pasta al limone
gremolata

lemongrass smoked+infused pork tenderloin

2 pork tenderloins, 1½ lbs. each, frozen
1 tsp. finely ground black pepper
1 Tbl. fine sea salt
3-4 Tbl. olive oil (used with grilling and for searing/sautéing, not oven cooking)
5-6 stalks lemongrass

1) Cut lemongrass stalks into 6" long pieces and split them lengthwise. Quarter the larger diameter pieces. For grilling, soak in water for at least 2 hours or overnight.

2) Freeze the pork tenderloins separately, if possible, to allow maximum surface area for flavor infusion.

Grill version:

1) When ready to smoke, combine salt, black pepper, and olive oil in a zippered bag with the two pork tenderloins and rub the mixture to completely cover the meat. Let rest while grill is heating.

2) Set up the grill for offset grilling. The vents should be set to produce a temperature in the range of 250°F – 275°F.

3) When the coals are ready, place the lemongrass on the coals and wait a few minutes to start producing smoke. For a gas grill, follow instructions for smoking.

4) Place the pork tenderloins on the grill and cook until done, 2-3 hours. Remove from heat and let rest 10 minutes.

Oven version:
Preheat oven to 275°F.
1) Place cut lemongrass in the bottom of a casserole dish or baking pan large enough to hold the pork tenderloins and tall enough to at least reach the top of the pork. Add ¼" of water to pan.

2) Rub the frozen tenderloins with salt and pepper and place on top of lemongrass. Tightly seal the casserole or baking dish with aluminum foil.

3) Roast for 2-2½ hours or until done. For shredded pork, cook for an additional 30 minutes.

If the tenderloins were frozen together, after approximately 90 minutes separate them, salt and pepper the exposed sides. Place new sides down and continue cooking.

Both versions: if the tenderloin is too tender to slice, then shred it. Refrigerating overnight may make the tenderloin firm enough to slice.

Medallions: Slice tenderloin into 1" thick medallions. Add olive oil to a pan over medium to medium high heat and sear the two flat sides of the medallions to make them crispy. They're ready to flip (or remove) when they slide freely in the pan.

Shredded: Shred the whole tenderloin(s) or just the ends. Add olive oil to a pan over medium to medium high heat and sauté to make them crispy.

Makes 8 servings of two 1-inch medallions or 3-3½ cups of shredded pork.

pasta al limone

½ c. olive oil
½ c. grated parmesan or pecorino cheese
1 lemon, juiced and zest minced
salt and pepper to taste
1 lb. cooked pasta

Whisk together olive oil, cheese, lemon juice and zest, salt and pepper. Mix with cooked pasta.

Makes 1 lb. lightly sauced pasta.

gremolata

½ c. fresh parsley, basil, or oregano
zest of one lemon
1 clove garlic

Mince all ingredients together.

Makes ½ cup garnish/condiment.

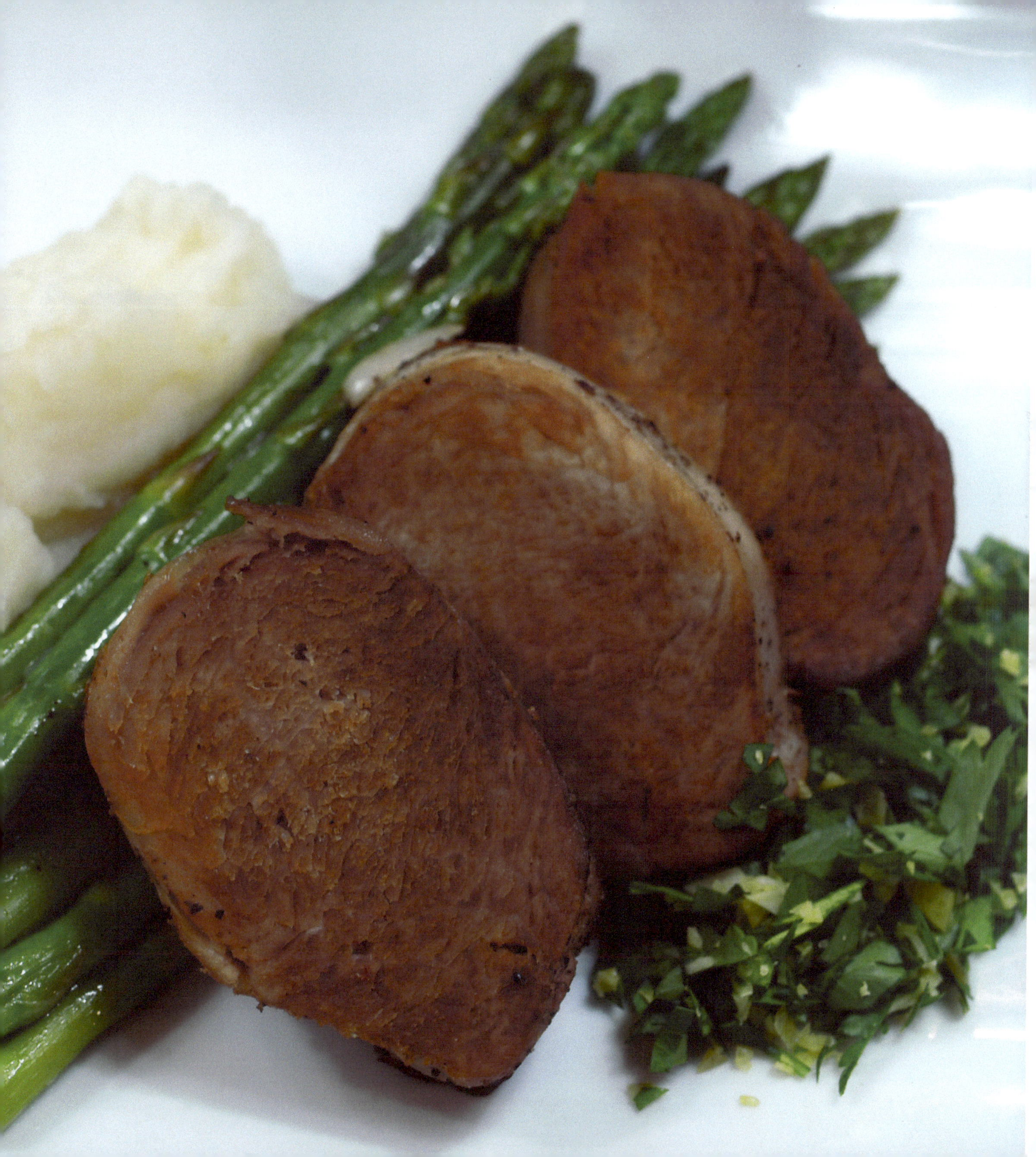

gradient

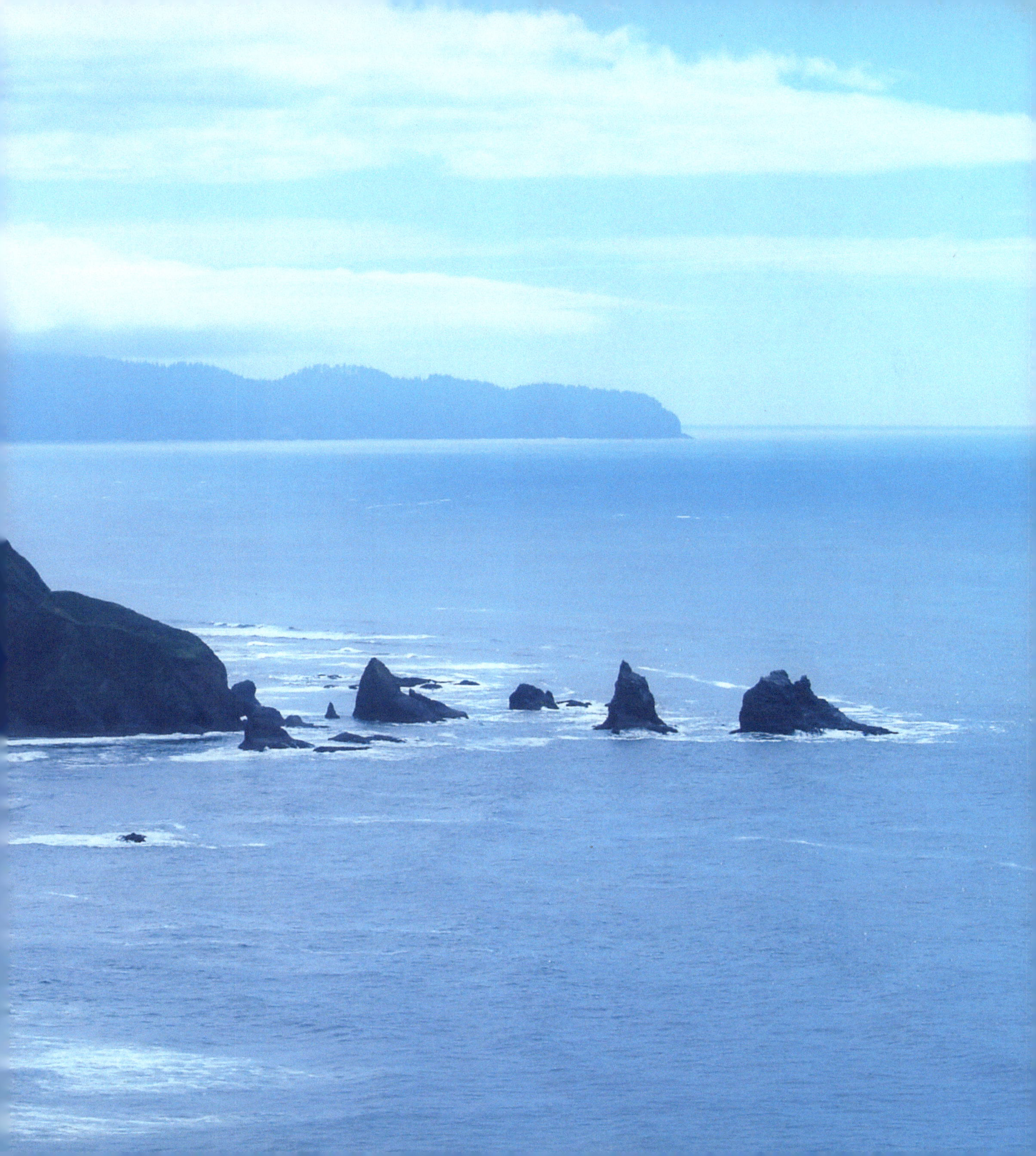

Storytelling is a wonderful way to share the moments of our lives, whether exciting adventures or every-day experiences, and telling those stories opens up worlds of new possibilities to explore in design, yarn, winemaking and life.

on pins & needles

Dive into a world of characters and locations and eras with colors as soft-spoken or intense as their namesakes.

The beautiful colors of Canon Hand Dyes are inspired by beloved classics like Don Quixote, The Canterbury Tales, and Peter Rabbit as well as modern favorites like My Neighbor Totoro, Harry Potter, and Downton Abbey. Colors that are as evocative as their namesakes: rich, whimsical, or capricious.

Based in Portland, Oregon, Amy Lee Sardell hand-dyes these gorgeous gradients, beautifully coordinated color work kits, and lively self-striping yarns on a variety of bases with names like William, Oscar, Charles, Lewis, Jane, Charlotte, and Emily, continuing the literary tradition.

The yarns of Canon Hand Dyes evoke a journey, a quest, an endeavor, an odyssey, and beautifully showcase stitches and design motifs.

Come with us and escape into the world of literary adventure.

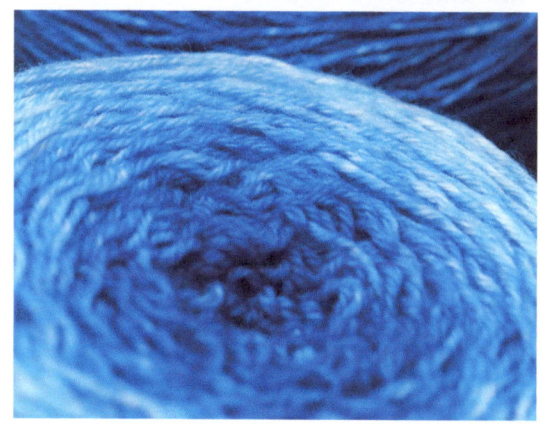

109

on the menu

Every good wine tells a story and those stories deliciously unfold at Adrice Wines. Winemaker Pam Adkins has a strong background in West Coast winemaking and loves to experiment, co-owner Julie Bulrice charmingly tells the stories, and together they form Adrice (pronounced "address").

Distinctive grape varietals and exploratory processes are elemental to Adrice Wines. Wonderful small-lot wines from non-traditional grape varietals—for a Washington State winery—like Baco Noir, Pinot Noir, Nebbiolo, and Montepulciano are a treat and favorites such as Cabernet Sauvignon, Merlot, and Syrah shine. The experiments include two small-batch Port-style dessert wines and a unique Syrah aged in Bourbon or Rye Whiskey barrels.

Affectionately named Fool's Gold, the Bourbon barrel-aged Syrah has multiple intertwined and shifting layers of aroma and flavor—the liquid equivalent of a color gradient. Swirling through vanilla and caramel to cherry, blackberry, and blueberry with hints of spice and dried orange peel. Wouldn't it make a lovely colorway? It certainly makes a lovely wine.

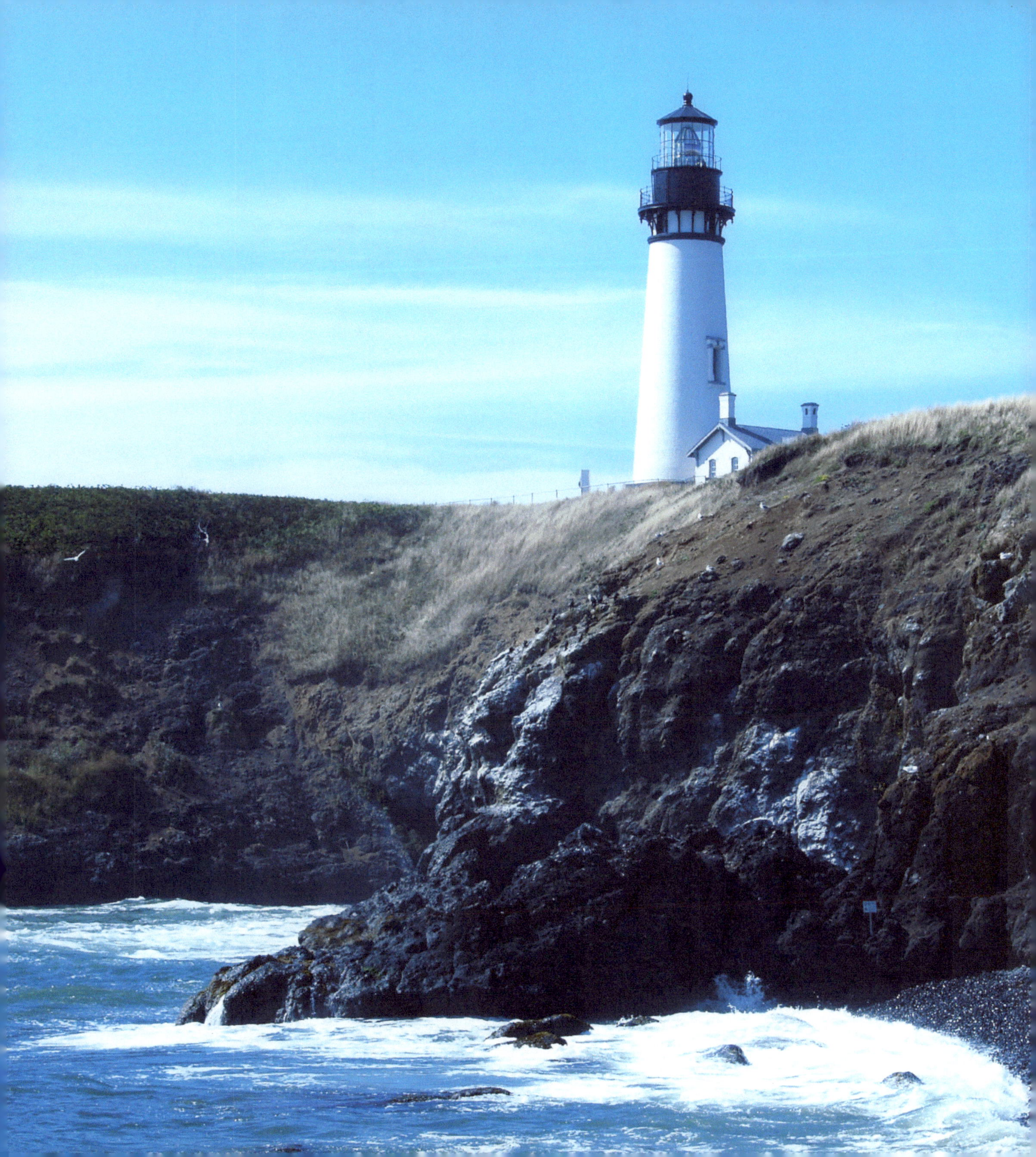

gradien

on pins & needles

Shape, texture, color—these are the three basic elements I gather when starting a new design—sometimes starting with all three at once and other times in a progression.

This shawl design was a progression, starting with the wave shape. I was fascinated by assymetrical increases and after playing around with different increase rates I realized that this curling shape was a lot of fun.

The stitch came next—I wanted a ripple-like stitch that could evoke water or flames or leaves and after deconstructing and experimenting with multiple lace patterns, decided on this one. The embellishments of cables and beads are an added bonus.

The color decision came last, but certainly wasn't least. I initially envisioned this shawl in a solid or semi-solid yarn to show off the stitches, but once I saw Canon Hand Dyes gradients, I couldn't wait to see how this shawl would work with gradient yarn—I'm so happy that I tried it!

I hope you enjoy knitting this shawl as much as I enjoyed designing it.

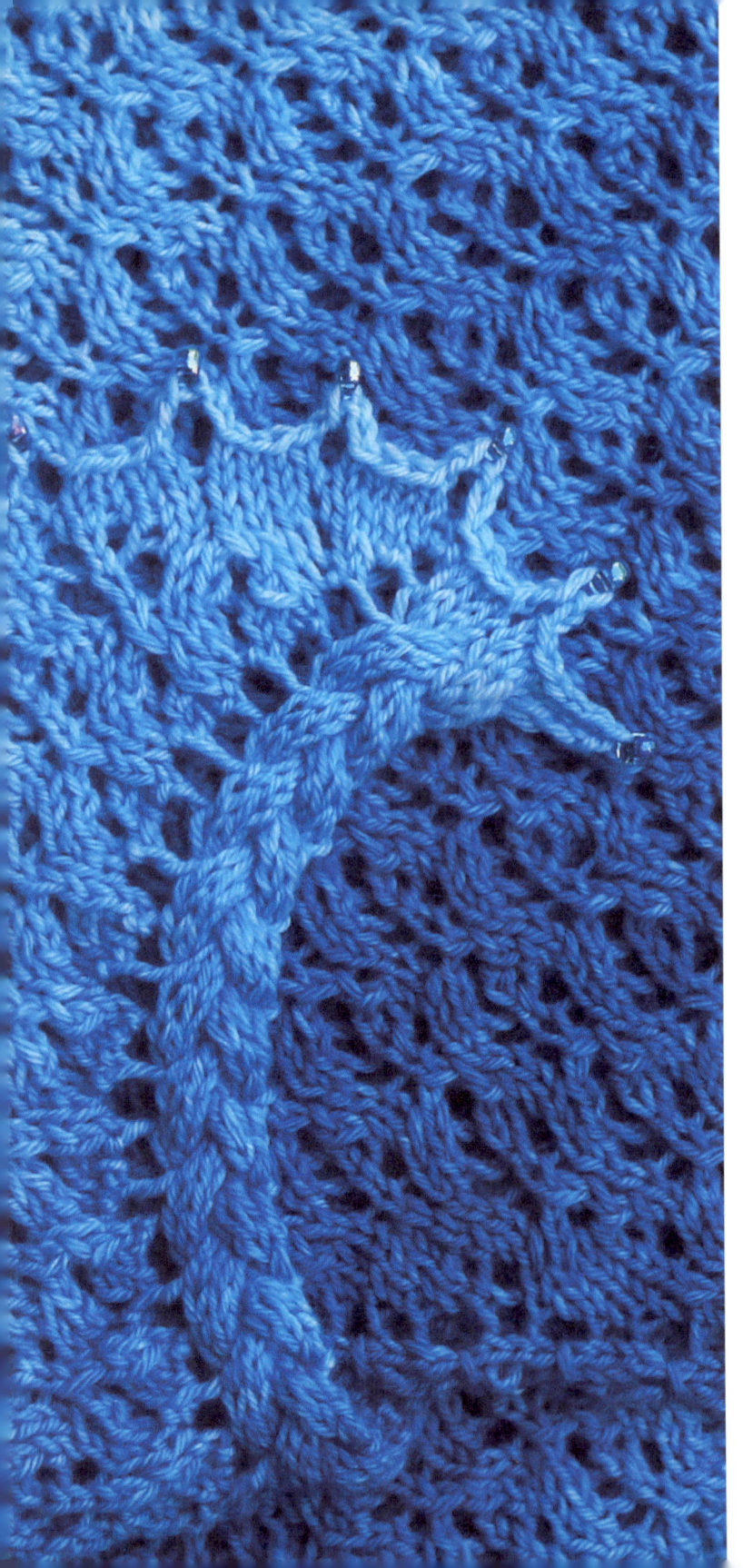

sunspray

Size
Overall 57" wingspan x 28" deep (145 x 70 cm) with 38" (95 cm) on straight (coin) side, 38" (95 cm) inside curve, and 79" (200 cm) outside curve; size is customizable.

Yarn
Fingering weight, approximately 920 yds.

Shown in Canon Hand Dyes William Merino Fingering (460 yds / 100 g), 2 gradient cakes in Blue Curaçao

Gauge and Needles
21 sts & 34 rows = 4" / 10 cm in lace pattern after blocking using US 1-5 (2.5-3.75 mm) or size needed to get gauge.

Gauge is not critical for this project; a different gauge will yield a different size and have different yarn requirements.

Notions
110 size 3 round beads and tiny crochet hook for placing beads (if substituting, bead should slide freely on yarn held doubled), cable needle, stitch markers (one removable), stitch holder, crochet hook (optional, for provisional cast on)

Stitches
For standard stitches, see page 128.

coin — slip the 3rd stitch on left needle over the first two stitches, knit 1, yarn over, knit 1 — st count remains the same

Instructions

Shawl is worked flat starting with a tab cast on and the wave form is shaped from the point outward. Braided and coin edges are worked at the same time as the lace pattern and beads are added in bind off.

Some knitters find it helpful to separate repeats with markers. Repeat marker positions will change on Rows 1, 3, 9, and 11; follow the chart or instructions and move markers as needed. These additional repeat markers are not included in the instructions. Instructions refer only to markers next to the braided and coin edges.

cast on and setup rows

[chart on page 116]

Provisionally **cast on** 3 sts.

Setup Row 1 (RS): K3.
Setup Row 2 (WS): P3.
Setup Row 3 (RS): K3.
Setup Row 4 (WS): P3.
Setup Row 5 (RS): P+k, k2 — 1 st inc, 4 sts total; place removable marker on first st.
Setup Row 6 (WS): P4.
Setup Row 7 (RS): K1, coin.
Setup Row 8 (WS): P4.
Setup Rows 9 (RS): K4.
Setup Row 10 (WS): P4.
Setup Row 11 (RS): K1, coin.

Unpick provisional cast on and place 3 sts on holder.

main section

setup rows

	knit on RS, purl on WS		coin	+ p+k	/ k2tog	⋏ sk2p		C6L		repeat
	provisional cast on		pick up & purl	○ yo	\ ssk			C6R		edge marker

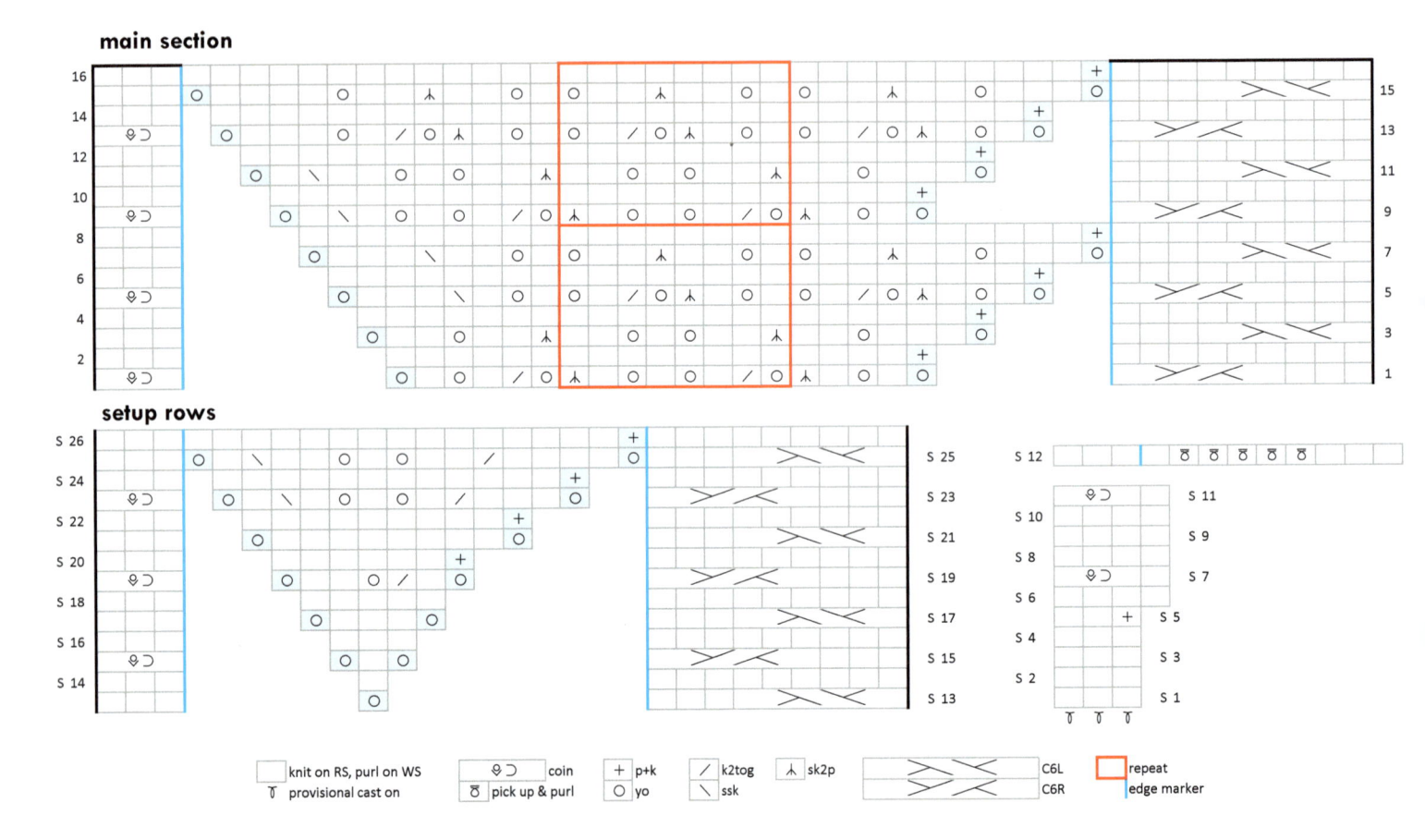

Setup Row 12 (WS): P3, pm, p1, rotate ¼ turn clockwise, pick up & purl 5 sts to row with removable marker, p3 from holder — 12 sts; remove removable marker.

Setup Row 13 (RS): C6L, k3, sm, yo, pm, k3 — 1 st inc, 13 sts.

Setup Rows 14, 16, 18 (WS): Purl.

Setup Row 15 (RS): K3, C6R, sm, yo, k1, yo, sm, coin — 2 sts inc, 15 sts.

Setup Row 17 (RS): C6L, k3, sm, yo, k3, yo, sm, k3 — 2 sts inc, 17 sts.

Setup Row 19 (RS): K3, C6R, sm, yo, k1, k2tog, yo, k2, yo, sm, coin — 2 sts inc, 19 sts.

Setup Rows 20, 22, 24 (WS): Purl to 1 st before last marker, p+k, sm, p9 — 1 st inc, 20, 23, 26 sts.

Setup Row 21 (RS): C6L, k3, sm, yo, k8, yo, sm, k3 — 2 sts inc, 22 sts.

Setup Row 23 (RS): K3, C6R, sm, yo, k3, k2tog, k1, yo, k1, yo, k1, ssk, k1, yo, sm, coin — 2 sts inc, 25 sts.

Setup Row 25 (RS): C6L, k3, sm, yo, k4, k2tog, k2, yo, k1, yo, k2, ssk, k1, yo, sm, k3 — 2 sts inc, 28 sts.

Setup Row 26 (WS): Purl to 1 st before last marker, p+k, sm, p9 — 1 st inc, 29 sts.

main section

[chart on page 116]

Row 1 (RS): K3, C6R, sm, [yo, k1] twice, sk2p, *yo, k2tog, [k1, yo] twice, k1, sk2p,* repeat between * to 4 sts before last m, yo, k2tog, [k1, yo] twice, sm, coin — 2 sts inc.

Row 2 and all WS rows: Purl to 1 st before last marker, p+k, sm, p9 — 1 st inc.
Row 3 (RS): C6L, k3, sm, yo, k3, yo, k2, *sk2p, k2, yo, k1, yo, k2,* repeat between * to 7 sts before last m, sk2p, [k2, yo] twice, sm, k3 — 2 sts inc.
Row 5 (RS): K3, C6R, sm, [yo, k1] twice, sk2p, yo, k2tog, k1, yo,* k1, yo, k1, sk2p, yo, k2tog, k1, yo,* repeat between * to 7 sts before last m, k1, yo, k1, ssk, k3, yo, sm, coin — 2 sts inc.
Row 7 (RS): C6L, k3, sm, yo, k3, yo, k2, sk2p, k2, yo, *k1, yo, k2, sk2p, k2, yo,* repeat between * to 8 sts before last m, k1, yo, k2, ssk, k3, yo, sm, k3 — 2 sts inc.
Row 9 (RS): K3, C6R, sm, [yo, k1] twice, sk2p, *yo, k2tog, [k1, yo] twice, k1, sk2p,* repeat between * to 8 sts before last m, yo, k2tog, [k1, yo] twice, k1 ssk, k1, yo, sm, coin — 2 sts inc.
Row 11 (RS): C6L, k3, sm, yo, k3, yo, k2, *sk2p, k2, yo, k1, yo, k2,* repeat between * to 11 sts before last m, sk2p, k2, yo, k1, yo, k2, ssk, k1, yo, sm, k3 — 2 sts inc.
Row 13 (RS): K3, C6R, sm, [yo, k1] twice, sk2p, yo, k2tog, k1, yo,* k1, yo, k1, sk2p, yo, k2tog, k1, yo,* repeat between * to 11 sts before last m, k1, yo, k1, sk2p, yo, k2tog, k1, yo, k3, yo, sm, coin — 2 sts inc.
Row 15 (RS): C6L, k3, sm, yo, k3, yo, k2, sk2p, k2, yo, *k1, yo, k2, sk2p, k2, yo,* repeat between * to 12 sts before last m, k1, yo, k2, sk2p, k2, yo, k4, yo, sm, k3 — 2 sts inc.
Row 16 (WS): Purl to 1 st before last marker, p+k, sm, p9 — 1 st inc.

Repeat Main Section Rows 1-16: 15 more times, ending on Row 15 (RS) — 69 coins total including setup section.

If customizing size, save the equivalent of at least 9 rows of yarn for finishing and bind off. Total stitch count should be a mulitple of 16 plus 14 sts.

Final Row 16 (WS): Purl to 1 st before last marker, p+k, turn work without working last 9 sts — 1 st inc, 463 sts.

beaded bind off and finishing
Bindoff Setup Row 1 (RS): Knit to last m, yo, sm, coin — 1 st inc, 464 sts.
Bindoff Setup Row 2 (WS): Purl to end of row.

*Chain (ch) can be crocheted or knitted. For each knitted chain st: *k1, place st back on left needle,* repeat between * for as many chain sts as needed.*

*Bind off by *ssk and placing stitch back on left needle,* repeat between * for as many bind off stitches needed.*

Bindoff: With right side facing, bo-1, *ch-2, place bead onto last st using tiny crochet hook, ch-2, bo-4,* repeat between * to last 4 sts, bo-3, ch-2, place bead onto last st using tiny crochet hook, ch-2, ssk. Break yarn and fasten off.

Weave in ends. Block.

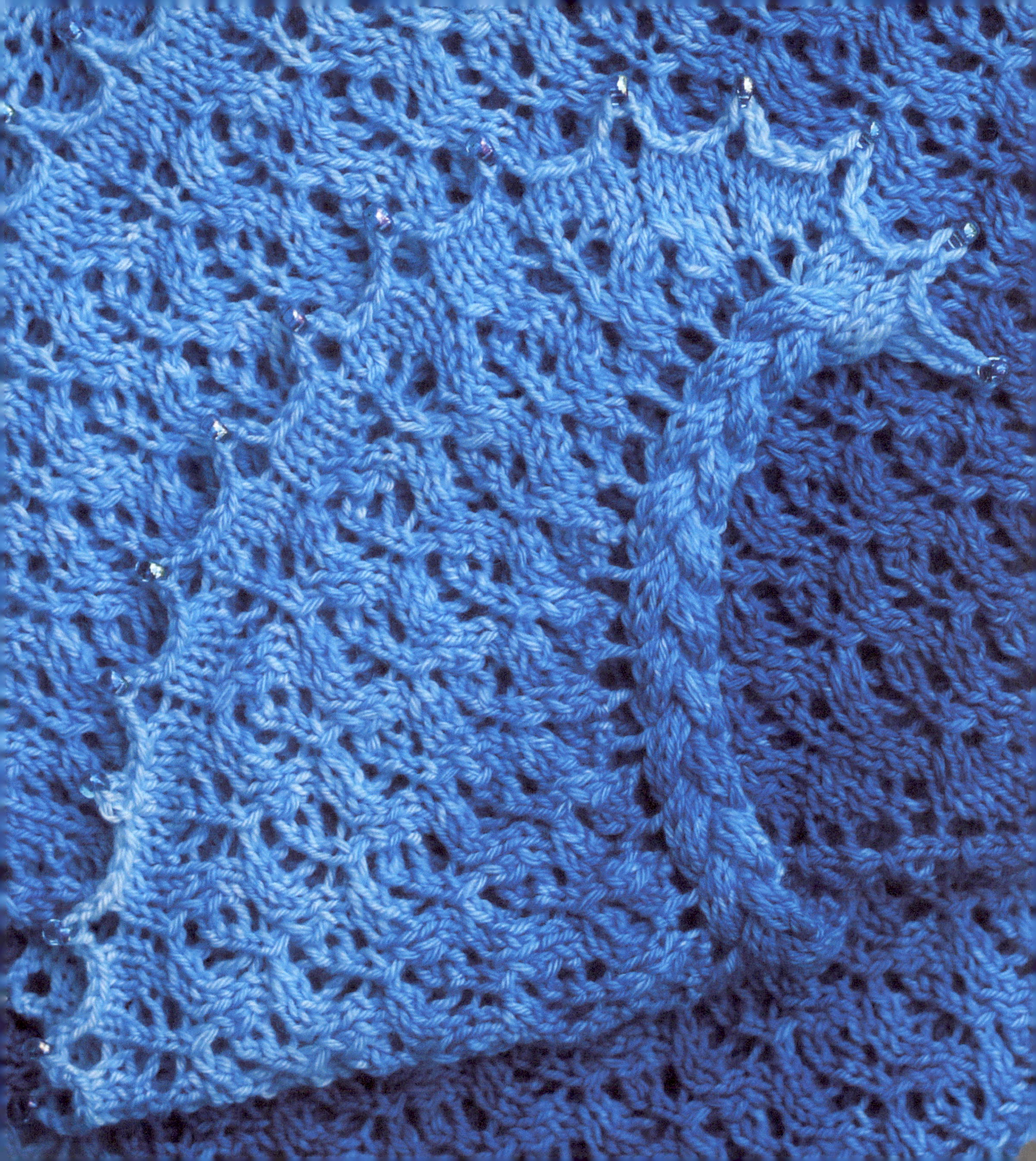

gradient

on the menu

Why is dessert always served last? Sometimes it might be nice to start with dessert, especially this simple and delicious blend of hot and cold, sweet and tart.

Citrus + ginger caramel and perfectly cooked creamy pears. Vanilla bean ice cream. Sugared citrus zest as an edible garnish. Simple and delicious.

Adrice Wines 2016 Fool's Gold Syrah is a truly unique wine. Bourbon barrel aging of this wine adds flavors and aromas of vanilla, caramel, smoke, and of course bourbon to the cherry, blackberry, and blueberry aromas and flavors of Washington State Syrah. Hints of spice and dried orange peel from the Syrah also provide a bridge from the wine to the dessert.

This wine has a complex interaction with the dessert, reinforcing the caramel and ginger flavors and providing a contrast of red and black fruit as a counterpoint to the citrus. Try it, we think you'll like it. We did!

food

citrus caramel pears (page 123)
vanilla bean ice cream
sugared citrus curls (page 124)

wine

Adrice Wines
2016 Fool's Gold
Bourbon barrel-aged Syrah

cooking & plating

1) Make citrus syrup 1 day in advance and refrigerate overnight.

2) Make citrus curls up to 1 day in advance and store in a cool dry place.

3) Make pears immediately before serving.

4) Place a scoop of vanilla ice cream onto plate.

5) Place pear onto plate and spoon caramel sauce over the top.

6) Garnish with sugared citrus curls.

Pears are also delicious served on top of sourdough waffles [page 19].

recipes

citrus caramel pears
sugared citrus curls

citrus caramel pears

4 ripe but firm pears; peeled, halved, cored
¼ lb. butter (1 stick)
1 c. granulated sugar
1 c. water
1 orange, juice and zest
1 lemon, juice and zest
1 lime, juice and zest
1"-1½" peeled ginger cut into ½" chunks

1) **Citrus syrup:** combine sugar, water, ginger, citrus juice and zest in a saucepan, bring to a boil, then reduce heat and simmer uncovered until reduced by half. Let cool, preferably overnight, then strain to remove zest and ginger, reserving the syrup.

2) Melt the butter in a sauté pan or skillet. Add pears flat side down and cook over medium high heat until brown. Flip onto round side and brown, then flip back to flat side.

3) Add citrus syrup and reduce heat to medium (it should still be bubbling). Continue cooking until the sauce is thickened and turns a light caramel color and the pears are done. Remove pears to serving plates before they get too soft; they are done when a sharp paring knife is easily inserted into the thickest part of the pear. If needed, continue to cook the sauce after removing the pears.

Makes 8 servings.

sugared citrus curls

fresh orange, lemon, lime
granulated sugar

1) If using a zester: zest the citrus fruits, being careful not to peel any of the white pith.

If using a vegetable peeler: peel strips of zest, being careful not to peel any of the white pith. Julienne the zest.

2) Place zest strips in a bowl or zippered plastic bag of sugar and cover bowl tightly or zip bag. Shake until curls are coated with sugar. Uncover bowl or open bag until ready to use.

3) Store overnight or up to 2 days in a cool, dry place. Zests will get crispier as they dry.

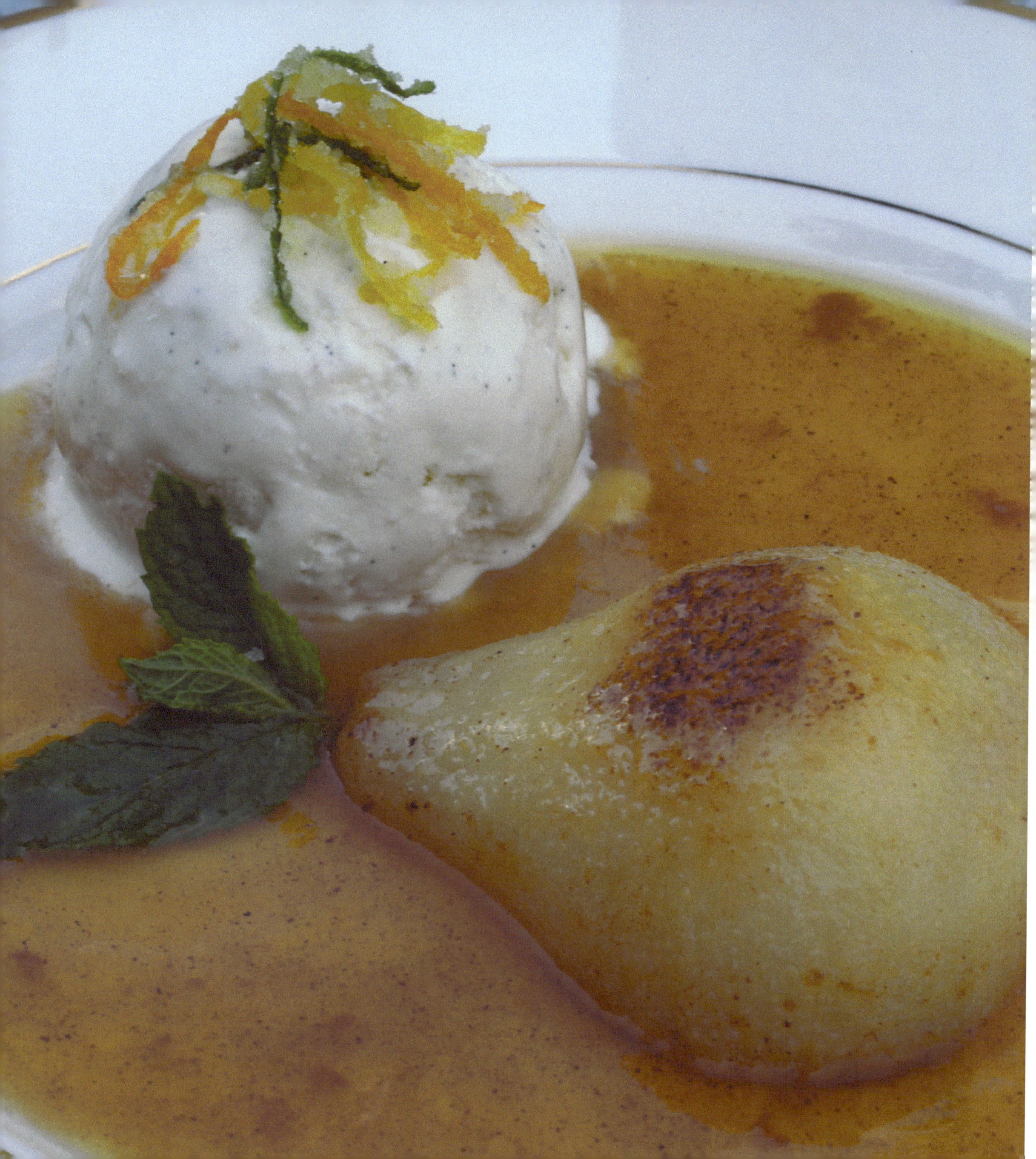

more

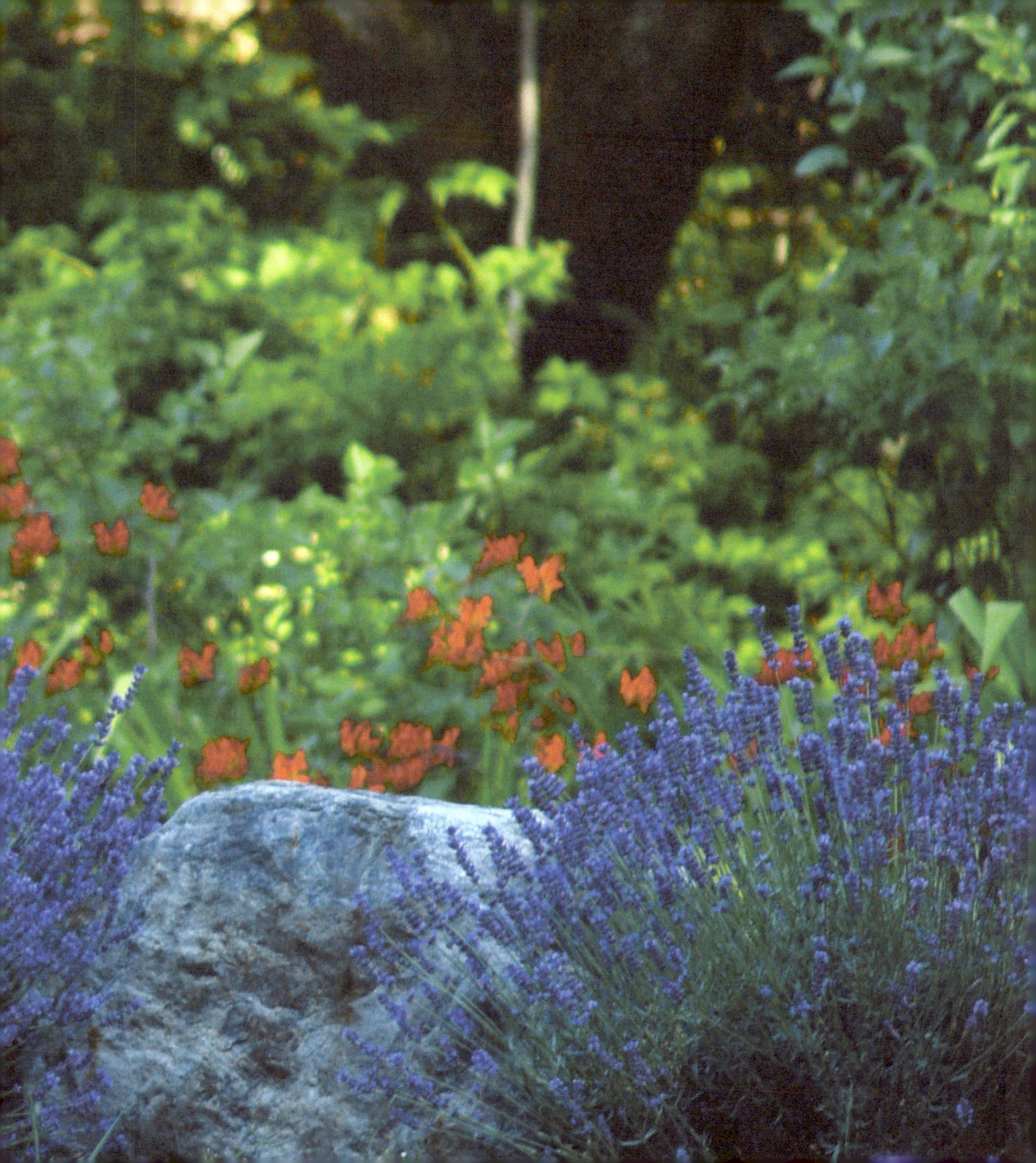

stitches + abbreviations

st(s) — stitch(es)
RS — right side
WS — wrong side
inc — increase
dec — decrease
tog — together
cn — cable needle
☐ repeat
| **m** — marker
pm — place marker
sm — slip marker
rm — remove marker
☐ **k** — knit on rs, purl on ws
— **p** — purl on rs, knit on ws
co — cast on
⍋ **provisional co** — provisional cast on

[...] # times, {...} # times — repeat the instructions between the [ ] or { } brackets for the number of times indicated

c1, c2 — color 1, color 2

k#-c1 / k#-c2 — knit the # of stitches with color 1 or color 2, e.g. k3-c1 means knit 3 with color 1

p#-c1 / p#-c2 — purl the # of stitches with color 1 or color 2, e.g. p1-c2 means purl 1 with color 2

work even — continue in established pattern without increasing or decreasing

stockinette — knit on right side, purl on wrong side

reverse stockinette — purl on right side, knit on wrong side

2x2 ribbing — *k2, p2,* repeat between * for length indicated in pattern

○ **yo** — yarn over

∨ **sl or sl yb** — slip with yarn in back

∀ **sl yf** — slip with yarn in front

psso — pass the slipped stitch(es) over the just worked st(s)

-tbl — -through back loop(s)

k-tbl — knit through back loop

p-tbl — purl through back loop

k2tog — knit 2 together

k2tog-tbl — knit 2 tog through back loops

p2tog — purl 2 together

k3tog — knit 3 together

p3tog — purl 3 together

p4tog — purl 4 together

ssk (slip slip knit) — sl-2 sts individually knitwise, place back on left needle, knit both sts together tbl; same result as skp (sl-1, k1, psso)

ssp (slip slip purl) — sl-2 sts individually purlwise, place back on left needle, purl both sts together tbl

sk2p (slip k2tog psso) — sl-1 st knitwise, knit 2 tog, pass slipped stitch over (2 sts dec)

p+k (purl and knit) — purl and knit into the same stitch (1 st inc)

M **M1R (make 1 right)** — pick up strand between stitches and place it on left needle, knit into the front loop

M **M1L (make 1 left)** — pick up strand between stitches and place it on left needle, knit into the back loop

M1p (make 1 purlwise) — pick up strand between stitches and place it on left needle, purl into the front loop

C3/1R (cable 3/1 right) — sl-1 to cn and hold to back of work, k3, k1 from cn

C3/1L (cable 3/1 left) — sl-3 to cn and hold to front of work, k1, k3 from cn

X3/1R (cross 3/1 right) — sl-1 to cn and hold to back of work, k3, p1 from cn

X3/1L (cross 3/1 left) — sl-3 to cn and hold to front of work, p1, k3 from cn

C4R (cable 4 right) — sl-2 to cn and hold to back of work, k2, k2 from cn

C4L (cable 4 left) — sl-2 to cn and hold to front of work, k2, k2 from cn

C6R (cable 6 right) — sl-3 to cn and hold to back of work, k3, k3 from cn

C6L (cable 6 left) — sl-3 to cn and hold to front of work, k3, k3 from cn

⌳ **C6R-dec (cable 6 right with a decrease)** — sl-3 sts to cable needle and hold to back, k2tog, k2, k3 from cable needle—1 st dec

⌳ **C6R-inc (cable 6 right with an increase)** — sl-3 sts to cable needle and hold to back, k3, p+k first st from cable needle, k2 from cable needle—1 st inc

⌳ **C8R (cable 8 right)** — sl-4 to cn and hold to back of work, k4, k4 from cn

⌳ **C8L (cable 8 left)** — sl-4 to cn and hold to front of work, k4, k4 from cn

✳ **supernova** — slip 5 sts to right needle as if to purl, dropping YOs; slip same 5 sts back to left needle; keeping original 5 sts on left needle until stitch is complete {knit 5 together - yo - knit the same 5 sts tog - yo - knit the same 5 sts tog} all into the same 5 sts — stitch count remains the same

↓ **knit with loose strands** — with left needle tip at back of work, lift the strands carried by slipped stitches of 2 previous rows onto left needle, knit the loose strands from previous 2 rounds together with the next stitch — stitch count remains the same

← **move stitches left (new beginning of round)** — move number of stitches indicated to the left by removing the marker, slipping number of sts indicated, and replacing marker for new beginning/end of round

coin — slip the 3rd stitch on left needle over the first two stitches, knit 1, yarn over, knit 1 — st count remains the same

bo (bind off) — *k2tog, replace stitch back on left needle,* repeat between * for number of sts indicated

SSK bo (SSK bind off) — *ssk, replace stitch back on left needle,* repeat between * for number of sts indicated

purl bind off — *p2tog, replace stitch back on left needle,* repeat between * for number of sts indicated

ch (chain) — chain st can be crocheted or knitted. For each knitted chain st: *k1, place st back on left needle,* repeat between * for as many chain sts as needed

● **B (place bead)** — work stitch and place it back on left needle, pick up bead on tiny crochet hook, hook the stitch just worked and slide bead onto stitch, place stitch on right needle (if no stitch is indicated, work stitch as knit 1 and then place bead on it)

gratitude

A book like this is certainly not an individual effort and we appreciate all of the encouragement and support given to us along the way.

To all of our family, friends, teachers, producers, and supporters — we thank you for our shared history, experiences, and lessons.

To all the people we meet on our knitting, yarn, wine, and food adventures — we thank you for so generously sharing your stories and providing inspiration.

To all of the folks that directly contributed to the successful production of this book — thank you!

First and foremost, thank you to **Kevin Gehringer**, chief flavorologist and amazing photographer, without whom this book would not be possible. Kevin provided the **gorgeous photography, amazing recipes,** and **brilliant wine pairings** along with the loving support for my creative adventure.

Thank you to our fantastic **test knitters** Carol Buchmilller, Heather Gibbs, Shannon Daughtrey, and Susannah Iltis for their meticulous attention to detail.

Thank you to our absolutely stunning **models**, sisters Laila Albernaz and Lina Albernaz, for making the knitwear look so beautiful.

Thank you to our adventurous **recipe tester** Monica Catunda and her family for sharing culinary skills and taste buds.

Thank you to our lovely **production assistant** Lina Albernaz for cheerfully lending a hand with photo shoots.

Thank you to additional photographers for capturing the beauty and joy of knitting and wine. The majority of the photos in this book were captured by Kevin Gehringer, with additional images generously provided by LaVonne Stucky / The Wool Mill at Serenity Sheep Farm [pg 65, 66, 67, 69]; Billly Farrow [pg 67]; Veronika Jobe / YOTH Yarns [pg 133 - jalousie].

...and **to you, our readers,** *thank you for being interested in knitting and wine and food and taking the time to pursue your own creative adventure.*

links

Thank you to all of the amazing people and companies that make by hand the wonderful products that appear in this book.

Adrice Wines — unusual varietals and unique processes combine to make distinctive award-winning and crowd-pleasing wines
Woodinville, WA; adricewines.wine

The Artful Ewe — artfully hand-dyed and hand-painted yarn and fibers in a warm, inviting, creative space that welcomes the community to knit, spin, investigate, and share
Port Gamble, WA; www.theartfulewe.com

Canon Hand Dyes — yarns inspired by literature including lovely gradients, lively self-striping and subtle semi-solid colors
Portland, OR; www.canonhanddyes.com

Damsel Cellars — a boutique winery specializing in big, bold reds of the Columbia Valley...hold in your heart the romance, the ritual, and the history of wine
Woodinville, WA; www.damselcellars.com

Dusted Valley — family grown and produced world-class wines from the Walla Walla Valley
Walla Walla + Woodinville, WA; www.dustedvalley.com

Full Pull / Block Wines — offering boutique wines of the world with special focus on the Pacific Northwest
Seattle + Wapato, WA; www.fullpullwines.com

The Homestead Hobbyist — amazing and unusual fiber blends, fabulous hand-dyed yarn and fiber
Seattle, WA; www.thehomesteadhobbyist.com

grist creative — design, knit, weave, yarn, wine, food: *life is a creative adventure*
Redmond, WA; www.gristcreative.com

NanoStitch Lab — unique hand-dyed yarns with colorways inspired by women in STEM and all aspects of science: astronomy, biology, chemistry, geology and more
Seattle, WA; nanostitchlab.com

The Wool Mill at Serenity Sheep Farm — Lovely sheep, gorgeous yarns, wonderful hospitality and farming; respecting the homesteading roots of the Gallatin Valley
Belgrade, MT; thewoolmill.com

Sparkman Cellars —
Family. Good Livin'. Damn Fine Wine.
Woodinville, WA; www.sparkmancellars.com

Sonoris Wines — acute sensory focus on aroma and flavor directs a winemaking style drawing inspiration from family to make great wines
Richland, WA; www.facebook.com/sonoriswines

if you enjoyed this book, you may also like these books and patterns by susan gehringer

Learn more at www.gristcreative.com

life is a *creative* adventure

CPSIA information can be obtained
at www.ICGtesting.com
Printed in the USA
LVHW01n2303240818
587968LV00002B/2/P